# Old MacDonald's
# Factory Farm

# C. DAVID COATS

# Old MacDonald's Factory Farm

## The Myth of the Traditional Farm and the Shocking Truth About Animal Suffering in Today's Agribusiness

**Foreword by DR. MICHAEL W. FOX**

CONTINUUM · NEW YORK

1991

The Continuum Publishing Company
370 Lexington Avenue
New York, NY 10017

Printed in the United States of America

*Library of Congress Cataloging-in-Publication Data*

Coats, C. David.
    Old MacDonald's factory farm : the myth of the traditional farm
and the shocking truth about animal suffering in today's agribusiness
/ C. David Coats ; foreword by Michael W. Fox.
       p.   cm.
    Bibliography: p.
    ISBN 0-8264-0439-1; ISBN 0-8264-0494-4 (pbk)
    1. Livestock factories—Moral and ethical aspects.   2. Animals,
Treatment of.   I. Title.
SF140.L58C63   1989                                    88-35325
179.3—dc19                                             CIP

This book is printed on recycled paper.

This book is dedicated to my parents,
Jackie and Betsan, who put me on the road,
and to my children, Mercedes and James,
who are still on it.

# Contents

# Foreword

At the tender age of three-and-a-half, my daughter Mara is already aware of what kinds of food she eats. She announced one evening that she was going to have Thanksgiving dinner with some of her mother's friends and they were going to have turkey. I told her that a turkey is a bird and that a bird is an animal. "We don't eat animals," she replied at once. However, when she went to the dinner she was told that it was alright to eat the turkey "because a farmer had killed it."

Adults will go to all kinds of measures to avoid their own discomfort and guilt, if any, over eating animals, including justifying the consumption of animals that have been raised and killed for them. A common justification is that God made animals for us to eat. But in the Bible it is quite clear that it was only after the fall of humanity that meat eating was condoned. Other reasons, based more on blind cultural traditions and false notions about diet and nutrition, include endorsing meat consumption because it is essential for one's health, virility, growth, and strength. Yet many children have an aversion to eating meat. Perhaps the wisdom of their bodies is telling us something that we should not dismiss as some childish phobia or sentimental attachment to baby lambs and chicks. The documentation in this book clearly raises some very basic questions in this regard, leading to the conclusion that a reduction in meat consumption, if not vegetarianism, is enlightened self-interest.

My daughter, Camilla, became a vegetarian some twelve years ago, seven years ahead of me. At eight years of age, she was clear in her mind that it was wrong to kill animals for food when we have all kinds of nutritious alternatives to eat. Plus, she "hated" the taste and texture of meat. Her brother, Mike Jr., two years her senior, decided to cut back on meat consumption, giving up the beloved hamburger, for health reasons. As a varsity athlete he had learned that complex carbohydrates were better for him than meat, especially before any competitive event or training session rowing with his crew team.

Thousands of young people now think twice about eating hamburgers because they come from dairy cows that, as this book shows, burn out by three to four years on the dairy factory farm: and from meat imported from South America and Australia, where the destruction of forests to open up land to raise cattle is now accelerating the spread of deserts and contributing to the greenhouse effect. The hamburger is becoming a symbol of global ecological destruction and environmental degradation. Likewise, as this book documents, the beef steak, once a symbol of affluence and a mark of national pride, is becoming synonymous with conspicuous consumption and waste.

The hungry world of over 5 billion people cannot be fed by an inefficient and wasteful meat-based agriculture. But there is hope if there is a reduction in the production and consumption of meat by the peoples of less economically and environmentally impoverished nations. Such a reduction, which is essential if these nations are to be able to feed their own people a few generations from now, is an integral part of what is called *sustainable* agriculture. As this book shows, a meat-based agriculture is not sustainable because non-renewable resources—land, topsoil, water, and fossil fuels—are squandered to raise food primarily for farm animals and not for people. With a sustainable agriculture, which is the modern, scientific term for organic or eco-agriculture, food surpluses could be provided to needy nations rather than being converted into meat. Wildlife and their habitats would also benefit since less land would be taken over to raise livestock and fewer, if any, dangerous pesticides would be used.

Readers will find the factual details in this book of how farm animals are treated on modern factory farms disturbing, if not unbelievable. But they are not exaggerated. This is not to say that farmers are deliberately cruel. They have become caught up in the same cruel economic treadmill as the poor animals themselves where the profitability of livestock and poultry farming is linked unwisely with the adoption of intensive, factory-like confinement systems: and with a dependence upon drugs to control disease and boost productivity to such an extent as to have become a recognized consumer health hazard.

Genetic engineering biotechnology is now being applied to various sectors of agriculture to increase the productivity, growth, and disease resistance of both plants and animals. If it is not applied prudently and integrated with the principles and science of sustainable agriculture and is used instead to consolidate and expand meat-based agriculture and ecologically unsound monoculture farming practices (including agroforestry), then it will fail. Using genetically engineered hormones to make pigs grow faster and cows produce even more milk, and vaccines, so that even more animals can be crowded together, is a misapplication of this technology. The wisdom of making various crops resistant to herbicides and to produce their own insecticides is also to be questioned. But using this technology to increase the nutrient value and climatic adaptability of various plant crops could mean a reduction in the acreage needed to produce food efficiently and thus help feed the hungry world.

Farm animals, plants, and the land are ours only in sacred trust. We violate this trust when we treat these living resources merely as commodities. This profane attitude is now lending to the commoditization and desacralization of the Earth and all its processes and elements. Indeed the natural world is fast becoming an industrialized, polluted, and dysfunctional wasteland. It is therefore enlightened self-interest for all involved in the biggest industry of all, agriculture, to bring an attitude of reverence for all life to bear upon the choices we make in terms of what we eat, what foods are produced, and what farming methods are practiced. A more enlightened compassionate humanity will look back upon these times of widespread abuse of the earth and cruelty toward animals with disbelief and sorrow. Old MacDonald's Factory Farm will be a thing of the past, a monument to human arrogance, indifference, ignorance, and greed, like the "satanic mills" of the industrial revolution that poet and artist William Blake saw poisoning and defiling God's creation. This book is a major step toward a new vision of a humane planetary stewardship which will become a reality only if we begin to make the right choices now, based upon the ethic of respect and reverence for all life and upon *ahimsa*, the avoidance of causing harm to other living things. Agriculture, like any other human industry, based upon these cardinal principles, will do much to heal the planet and ourselves in the process. We do not own the land; it is entrusted to us for the future children of the Earth.

Dr. Michael W. Fox
Vice President, The Humane Society of the
United States
Director, Center for Respect of Life and Environment,
Washington, D.C.

November 1988

# Preface

Isn't man an amazing animal? He kills wildlife—birds, kangaroos, deer, all kinds of cats, coyotes, beavers, groundhogs, mice, foxes, and dingoes—by the million in order to protect his domestic animals and their feed. Then he kills domestic animals by the billion and eats them. This in turn kills man by the million, because eating all those animals leads to degenerative—and fatal—health conditions like heart disease, kidney disease, and cancer. So then man tortures and kills millions more animals to look for cures for these diseases. Elsewhere, millions of other human beings are being killed by hunger and malnutrition because food they could eat is being used to fatten domestic animals. Meanwhile, some people are dying of sad laughter at the absurdity of man, who kills so easily and so violently, and once a year sends out cards praying for "Peace on Earth."

C. D. C.

# Acknowledgments

My most heartfelt gratitude is due to those who helped and supported this project:

Michael Fox especially for his powerful and inspiring introduction, and his photos. Cleveland Amory for his support. Nathaniel Altman for his encouragement at the beginning. Jim Mason for his photos and for having written with Peter Singer the book that inspired me, *Animal Factories*. Jon Wynne-Tyson for putting together *The Extended Circle*. Mike Irwin for his generous professional expertise and Donald Barnes, Alex Hershaft, Ann Baldwin, and Narca Moore for looking over the manuscript. Nancy Palmer for letting me use her library of children's books. In England, Peter Roberts, Joyce D'Silva, and Carol Long at Compassion in World Farming, Clare Druce at Chickens' Lib, and Hilly Bevan at Animus. Nicole Lambert, and Mme. Gilardoni in Paris, Wim J. de Kok in the Netherlands, Marjorie Spiegel in Austria, and all those around the world who assisted in many ways with photos, advice, and information, especially: Henry Rasof, Toni Hopman, Pam Clarke, Diane Halverson, Michael Klaper, Laurie Saunders, Keith Akers, Virginia Krouse, Brad Miller, and others.

Many thanks also to Michael Leach at Crossroad/Continuum whose children thought this should be a book and to Kyle Miller who agreed. And of course to the serendipitous Patti Breitman.

But most of all, more than thanks go to my wife, Peggy, who edited and proofread it all several times, heard it all many more times, and still stayed her loving, compassionate self.

Fig. 1.

# 1

# Factory Farming and You

Children learn about farm animals from pictures in storybooks. Scores of books on farm life have been published, many with beautiful illustrations or photographs. Most show individual animal families frolicking on the farm, or tell of farm animal life in the care of benevolent farmers. But developments in modern agriculture have left the storybook writer far behind. Not that he is unable to keep up to date; more likely, he is unwilling. There is little left in today's animal husbandry methods which is suitable, pleasant, or picturesque enough for him to illustrate for young readers.

## The "Old MacDonald" Image

Children's books idealize animal life on the farm with illustrations of idyllic barnyard scenes: pigs snoozing under a canopy of green trees, rolling in muddy puddles and rooting busily for acorns; calves frolicking in lush clover while their mothers graze close by or lie contentedly chewing the cud; and mother hens in the farmyard teaching their chicks to scratch for bugs and worms, as the rooster struts about ever watchful for danger. Stories set on farms with animals as major characters, like Wilbur, the pig in E. B. White's *Charlotte's Web,* and the nursery favorite, the Little Red Hen, TV cartoons, "model farms" at zoos and theme parks, and advertising using anthropomorphized animals, encourage the child to identify with animals and reinforce this charming image of farm life. Such images fixed in childhood are hard to reverse; for many adults, Old Mac-Donald, that jovial character with his farm full of happy animals, is still the model for animal-farming techniques.

The vast majority of domestic animals, however, do not lead this

idealized farm life. In fact, of the six billion animals slaughtered in the
US each year for food, only a handful live and die outside the
oppression of high-volume, high-tech modern farming.

The growth of agribusiness has completely transformed both crop
farming and animal raising. We are all aware of some of the fundamental changes in agriculture over the last seventy-five years—the
horsedrawn plow is long gone and even the traditional tractor has been
superseded by giant equipment. We have become familiar with forma-
tions of harvesters trailing away into the distance on vast prairie farms
with thousands of productive acres in corn and wheat. But how many
of us know the truth of modern animal-raising methods? How many
have seen pictures of large pig "factories" with hundreds of pregnant
sows chained up in rows of individual steel-barred cages, or experi-
enced the choking, dusty interiors of laying-hen battery barns with
sixty thousand squawking chickens stuffed five all together into little
wire cages. Certainly the truths and consequences of animal food mass
production—the methods, the health risks, the environmental effects,
and the ethics—are not made readily available to us, neither as
children nor as grown-ups.

*What as Christians do we believe about man's
relations to nature? . . . What, for instance, of the
abominations of factory farming? We are sent back
to the classic doctrine of man and nature found in
the 8th Psalm. The psalmist describes how man is
given a lordship over nature, to rule it and to use it;
a lordship which has grown in ways the psalmist
never dreamed. But it is a lordship neither absolute
nor arbitrary, but under God's own sovereignty
and will. Man and Nature are together parts of one
whole pattern of creation together serving the glory
of God.*

The Archbishop of Canterbury, the Right Reverend
Michael Ramsey, quoted in *Agscene* October 1985

Wittingly and unwittingly, children and adults are insulated from the
grim realities of factory farming. One hundred and fifty years ago,
most people lived in closer contact with rural life. Cities were much
smaller, many farms existed close by, and it was not unusual for herds
of cows, pigs, and sheep to be kept almost within the city limits. In

addition, many city families kept hens and roosters for eggs and meat. In those bygone days, nursery books more accurately reflected the agricultural scene.

Urban children today have little chance to see animals in traditional surroundings, except perhaps in the contrived and stylized "farms" at zoos and theme parks. Cities are larger and trips into the countryside reveal very few animals running around the barnyard. Children learn about farm animals from books, which tell the idealized story of old-fashioned farming bliss. Few children's books touch on modern intensive methods of raising animals, and none is explicit about their actual living conditions—nor about their ultimate fate. Even those children's books published by such industry organizations as The National Live Stock and Meat Board give no clear visual images of factory-farm conditions. There is nothing romantic or endearing about the factory farm.

## The Business of Factory Farming

In real life, scenes of apparently benign peacefulness are now found only on small, family-owned and traditionally run farms that raise a variety of crops and keep a few cows, pigs, and chickens. Sadly, the last forty years have been economically disastrous for such mixed farms. In 1945 there were nearly 6 million farms; by 1987, there were less than 2.2 million. Many small farmers have been forced to quit, while others have learned to specialize, concentrating on one type of animal, or one or two crops. As former Secretary of Agriculture Earl Butz put it, they had to "get big, or get out."

The industrialization of agriculture has been spurred on by the search for greater profits from the growing population's need for more food. Western countries, richer since World War II, now want more traditionally expensive meats and easily prepared processed foods. Beef, the current staple of the American diet in the form of hamburger and steak, outsold pork for the first time in the early 1950s, and chicken consumption has skyrocketed. The belief that high meat consumption is an essential ingredient of "the good life" has encouraged farmers and agribusinessmen to raise more, while still keeping it affordable to the millions enjoying the prosperity of the postwar period. Even though per capita beef consumption peaked in the late seventies, the growing population keeps production high. And the increased demand over the last forty years has been met by the development of a new style of farming; the mechanized, concentrated mass production of food animals in the factory farm.

How can there be so many chickens in the supermarket, you might ask, when you never see any running around? Beef cattle and dry dairy cows graze out in the fields, but where are the other animals? Those who know what to look for will recognize the long low buildings and tall feed silos clustered together, often surrounded by high barbed wire fences, as the homes of the modern farm animal. Visitors are discouraged on these intensive units because they upset the stressed animals or bring in diseases that can spread like wildfire.

The great majority of animals grown for food in industrialized countries—like the 6 billion animals slaughtered every year in the US alone—are raised in such intensive, high-volume farms with their purpose-built barns and specialized machinery. They are called factory farms because they have adopted mass-production techniques and modern business efficiency programs; the objective is to turn out high volumes of standardized product at minimal cost per unit. Not only traditional animals—dairy cows, pigs, beef cattle, sheep, chickens, and turkeys—are raised on factory farms. Businessmen have developed intensive systems to raise minks, silver foxes, alligators, frogs, turtles— and many other animals whose skins or bodies can be sold for profit.

Agribusinessmen favor factory farming because the compact operation greatly reduces two of their major expenses—land and labor. By concentrating animals into small areas, less land is needed; by automating many of the daily chores, labor is kept to a minimum. Additionally, the close confinement of the animals allows the operator to monitor constantly their various feeding, growing, and breeding functions.

The operator's close control over his stock and all aspects of the "raising" process means the operation can be managed in terms of accepted business practices and goals. All elements of input and output can be regulated towards greater profits. After all, factory farm operators—and agricorporations—are not in business simply to produce food; they are in business to make money. The more pigs an operator can raise on his facility, the more he can sell. The more efficient the sows are at turning feed and housing into piglets, the more money he will make.

To this end all is fair; animals cease to be treated as individual living creatures—and traditional animal husbandry ethics are ignored. Factory animals may be subjected to any procedure at all if it increases overall productivity. Even normal factory-farm conditions are horrific; cramped incarceration; mutilations; lack of sun and light; lack of exercise; chaining and caging; drugging; force-feeding and, paradoxically in the case of calves, deliberate malnutrition; forced weaning;

forced insemination; loss of individuality; general deprivation; frustration of natural instincts and the denial of freedom to express their normal behavior patterns. In this game it is perfectly okay to push animals to the very limits of their capacity—and beyond.

*Whenever people say "We mustn't be sentimental," you can take it they are about to do something cruel. And if they add "We must be realistic," they mean they are going to make money out of it.*

Brigid Brophy, *Don't Never Forget*

Nevertheless, while trade magazines tell the factory manager how to extract more from the animals, industry publications aimed at the general public volunteer little information about the abusive conditions and techniques. They obscure the reality of extreme confinement and outrageous treatment behind self-serving, semi-scientific, and commercial terminology. In fact, some insist that animals are better off in factory farms than in the old-fashioned barnyard or in the "dangerous" outdoors; they get regular food and water, their health can be checked, and they don't have to worry about predators. But these minimal needs are designed to benefit the farmer only, not the animals. They may bring about the fastest possible growth rate, but at the price of enduring pain for the animals.

Indeed, among all the factors of production, one is conspicuously missing from the factory farmers' equation: the right of every animal in human care to have, if not love and affection, then at least respect and consideration. Traditional farmers often knew their animals by name, gave care and attention to each, and had intimate knowledge of their individual needs and characteristics. They knew that animals living in fear of their human keepers are more susceptible to disease and injury, and more aggressive, and that this fear is only removed by compassionate and understanding contact. Like most sentient beings, animals thrive on affection—just like the family dog. But factory farmers have too many animals, and have neither the time nor the inclination to get to know them.

The concept of factory farming is intrinsically inhumane, because it denies animals their most basic rights as living beings. Old MacDonald certainly aimed to make a living on his farm, but he did not sacrifice his pride in traditional animal husbandry to coldly efficient and single-minded business principles. Now, humane treatment is seen as unnecessary, irrelevant, and in conflict with the maximization of profit.

When the bottom line is profit, compassion for animals goes out the window.

*In fact if one person is unkind to an animal it is considered to be cruelty, but where a lot of people are unkind to animals, especially in the name of commerce, the cruelty is condoned and, once large sums of money are at stake, will be defended to the last by otherwise intelligent people.*

Ruth Harrison, *Animal Machines*

## Factory Farming, World Food Politics, and the Environment

Man farms some 150 million tons of carcass meat every year, including chicken. The amount eaten in a year varies enormously from country to country, with well over 230 pounds per person consumed in the US and New Zealand, and less than 5 pounds for each man, woman, and child in India. The differences in quantities eaten in large part reflect the economic health of the various countries, but traditional eating habits, geography, and spiritual beliefs play their parts. India, for instance, and other Eastern countries have large populations that do not eat meat on religious and ethical grounds.

Factory farming is an inequitable and arbitrary use of the planet's available food, since this industry provides expensive and treasured grains to a favored few—inefficiently converted into meat by the domestic animal—while a hungry majority has too little to survive. Over three-quarters of Western grain crops are fed to animals, while in the Third World, many indigenous peoples cannot afford to buy their own local grain when faced with the competition of rich Western feed merchants. While hundreds of millions of tons of the world's grain harvest are fed to animals, less than 5 million tons of grains could provide adequate food for the 15 million children who starve to death each year.

The huge numbers of intensively raised domestic animals, forced into existence beyond their normal level of reproductivity by man's technological and genetic manipulation, are not helping to feed those in need, despite industry claims. These animals are, in fact, eating—and wasting—food that could be more equitably distributed among hungry people. When we note that it takes over twenty pounds of grain protein to produce just one pound of beef protein, we can begin to see the repercussions of our eating habits on the global food equation. Turning out more grain-fed beef fills the bellies of a few—but leaves many more with nothing to eat.

## The Environmental Consequences

From the environmental point of view, domestic animals destroy the lands they graze on and are a chief cause of the devastation of rain forest areas around the world. Indirectly they consume irreplaceable fossil fuels and water resources. When alive, factory animals' concentrated body wastes, laced with chemical residues, run off untreated into rivers and ground waters; when slaughtered, the processing of their bodies contributes again to water pollution.

Since World War II, grain farmers have heavily fertilized their land and sprayed herbicides, insecticides, and other chemicals in the struggle to increase production and make a living. Millions of acres of farmland topsoil have been reduced to an infertile powder that can only grow crops with the aid of an annual chemical fix. Water tables and wells all over the US have become undrinkable from years of pesticide contamination. Ultimately, the causes of this agricultural pollution are to be found not in the relatively few acres of cabbages, carrots, apples, and oranges, but in the intensive raising of grains and crops fed to intensively farmed animals. This rape of the land is a cost that will be borne by our children and their children.

And yet, ironically, as veterinarian and humanitarian Dr. Michael W. Fox—a noted opponent of factory farming—has written in *Farm Animals: Husbandry, Behavior, and Veterinary Practice,* "It is primarily because resources are being depleted and are becoming more costly, that farm animals must be raised under even more intensive efficiency-systems of industrialized production." Clearly, if the output and consumption of scarce and limited resources are becoming more costly and damaging to the long-term health of the planet, then we must look again closely at what we use them for. We must examine how human habits and behavior patterns affect our whole systems and we must reassess some of our basic "needs."

## Cost to Humans

One hundred and fifty years ago only the rich could afford to eat meat regularly. Most people lived on grains, bread, beans, vegetables, and dairy products, sometimes flavored with lard, ham bones, and stock.

With the advent of refrigeration in the late 1800s meat was brought in quantity and economically to population centers, and consumption began to rise. Since World War II, meat consumption per person has doubled in the US. Meat, once considered a luxury, is now plentiful and relatively cheap. It has become a staple food in the industrialized nations—though at enormous cost to the environment of the planet and the hungry of the world.

Medical and Western nutritional doctrine is based on a meat-centered diet because meat provides a concentrated source of daily protein in a readily available form. Research now shows our bodies' daily protein requirements are actually far less than was only recently supposed. Humans can get the protein they need from grains and other non-animal sources. Grains also provide necessary fiber or roughage in the diet—another reason, besides the inefficiency of grain-protein to meat-protein conversion, why eating the grain is healthier than eating the animals who have eaten the grain.

Meanwhile, children think of hamburger as a good food, "part of a nutritious meal." The dairy industry urges children to drink milk every day because, as the ads say, "it does a body good." And 75 percent of all the dishes on restaurant menus contain animal-based food with its saturated fat and cholesterol. Why is meat so in demand when high consumption of all animal foods is now conclusively linked to the increasing incidence of degenerative disease; heart disease, stroke, cancer, diabetes, arthritis, and many other problems?

Obviously, people eat meat because they like the taste, because they have been conditioned from childhood, and perhaps also because there is no sense of urgency to change; these diseases do not appear until later in life, even though the eating habits that cause them are set early. But men and women are being struck down younger and younger. Even six- and seven-year-old children have shown evidence of arterial plaque buildup, which can clog arteries and cause heart disease.

Tobacco was not banned when smoking was determined to be a cause of lung cancer; a lesson learned perhaps from the failed Prohibition Era in the US. But government warnings are now posted on advertising and cigarette packs, and smoking is increasingly banned in public and workplaces. In much the same way, there is clear epidemiological evidence that eating meat is directly connected to the degenerative diseases mentioned above. Why then is there no public acknowledgment of the health risks associated with eating meat? What keeps us from questioning this self-destructive convention? And where are the government warning labels?

While factory farming is only indirectly responsible for increased meat consumption and the resulting degenerative diseases, other insidious health problems hide in factory-farm meat. The Livestock Conservation Institute in the US has found that stress adversely affects the shelf life, flavor, and tenderness of meat because of its influence on muscle glycogen, lactic acid, and intracellular moisture levels—especially in pigs. If the psychological state of the food animal affects the quality of the meat—and dairy products from stressed cows must be included here—can factory-farm meat really be good for the humans that eat it? For certainly, after a lifetime of misery, a traumatic journey to the slaughterhouse and the terror of anticipated death, factory-farm animals are nothing if not stressed.

Drugs are given to animals on a regular basis to stimulate growth and to counter disease—among them antibiotics worth $300 million annually. These antibiotics are only a few of the thousands of drugs available from the $2 billion-a-year animal drug industry, which are injected and fed to animals. While the types of drugs given to animals are regulated, actual dosage given by individual operators is harder to control. For those who eat meat, the concern is that these drugs are not completely eliminated from the animals' bodies before they are killed; residues remain in the meat. Antibiotics given to human patients are less effective, ostensibly because of the exposure to antibiotics in the meat they have eaten.

A third worry concerns slaughtering and processing procedures. Chickens and other animals often have cancer and, even though the obvious tumors are cut off, the rest of their bodies may be processed and sold for human consumption. And the USDA has publicly acknowledged that 35 percent of slaughtered chickens may be contaminated with fecal matter and may cause salmonella poisoning—which can be fatal.

> *The calf that you carve with a smile is murder.*
> *And the turkey you festively slice is murder.*
> *Do you know how animals die?*
>
> The Smiths,
> from the title track of the album *Meat is Murder*

## Why This Book?

The factory-farming system essentially isolates the daily lives and consciousnesses of consumers from the birth-to-table processing of animals. Packaging and display techniques of supermarket meat complete the blurring of identification with the physical animal. The cruelties of factory-farm life hide unsuspected behind brightly colored packaging. Advertising messages use happy pigs to sell pork sausages, encouraging the customer to think all is well in pig world. TV ads show hamburgers growing on bushes. And what child would ever suspect that a wholesome funny clown could promote a food steeped in violence and cruelty?

As they grow older, small children are introduced to many new foods, including meats, fish, chicken, and dairy products, with names not obviously associated with the animals they come from. We have, in fact, one language for live animals, another for dead animals. Names of meats like pork, ham, bacon, pork sausages, lard, ribs, chops, beef, sirloin, ground beef, steak, hamburger, poultry, veal, nuggets, and drumsticks hardly reveal their origins. "Chicken" sounds like it comes from a chicken but, there may sometimes be a problem with identifying what is an animal and what is not. This terminology masks the source of the foods and children begin to eat them without knowing what they are or where they come from. Even some adults do not associate the food on their plate with the animal in the field—or on the factory farm.

*In point of fact, I am the very opposite of an anthropomorphizer. I don't hold animals superior or even equal to humans. The whole case for behaving decently to animals rests on the fact that we are the superior species. We are the species uniquely capable of imagination, rationality, and moral choice—and that is precisely why we are under the obligation to recognize and respect the rights of animals.*

Brigid Brophy, *Don't Never Forget*

Besides confusing meat names, our language hides the reality of dairy and egg production behind harmless euphemisms; cows "give" us milk and chickens "give" us eggs—as though they had a choice in the matter and were waiting gladly in line to pass over the goodies to their human benefactors. Phrases like we "get" beef from a cow, or bacon "comes from" a pig, give a small child the impression that somehow cattle and pigs willingly lay beef and bacon, just as hens lay eggs and cows make milk.

Later, even when it is understood that animals are killed for the meat, the methods of killing and the procedures of the slaughterhouse are barely acknowledged. In one industry pamphlet, a cartoon strip shows smiling cows entering the slaughterhouse; the next drawing shows a side of beef emerging. The cows have been miraculously, as the pamphlet says, "turned into" beef—without any unpleasantness. Can anything too grisly to describe be something we want to be a part of? Aren't we deliberately avoiding this horror by turning a conveniently blind eye?

Young children have a natural desire to play with animals, a tendency encouraged with stuffed bears and rabbits, pet dogs and cats, zoo trips, and many, many animal books. A child's love for fellow creatures is admired, and adults use animals to nurture feelings of love, tenderness, gentleness, and compassion. And in turn the child's love for animals is rewarded with love, tenderness, and approval from those around him.

*Do we have the right to rear animals in order to kill them so that we may feed appetites in which we have been artificially conditioned from childhood?*

Ashley Montague, *Of Man, Animals and Morals*

Then, confusion and bewilderment; the child is told it is okay to kill and eat the same animals he was just taught to love. He learns, often in consternation and distress, that cuddly lambs and playful piglets turn up at meal times, dead, and that he is expected to eat them. How does a child reconcile this conflict?

Some children feel revulsion for animal food when they find out exactly what it is. But most children, at first reluctant to eat meat, are cajoled or ridiculed into insensitivity. Our society believes this hardening of attitude toward the plight and destiny of domestic animals is just one of the lessons of growing up. Constant advertising, peer pressure, and frequent admonitions overwhelm the child; "it's what everybody does," "animals were put on earth for us to eat," "it says so in the Bible," and "it's God's will." The result is a numbing of compassion for animals. These weak and defenseless friends have somehow betrayed the child's love by allowing themselves to be killed and eaten—the dumb, stupid critters. Henceforth, food animals are rejected as appropriate objects of love—though the family dog is still a safe bet.

Small children seldom question the information that comes to them from parents, teachers, and books; they have no reason to. So, ingrained attitudes are forged in early childhood, and the message on animals is clear: loving and caring about animals is kid stuff—it's cute but you have to grow out of it. Animals exist only for man's benefit and have no rights themselves. They're just another throwaway item in a throwaway society.

Children's books, of course, attempt to foster love and care for animals by making them attractive, cute, and endearing. But even as they do so, telling the idealized story of traditional farming bliss, they unwittingly underscore the subtle, unwritten message that animals exist only to serve man's needs, that they have no rights other than those allotted to them by their keepers, that chickens exist to provide us with breakfast eggs, and cows are here to keep us in milk, butter, and cheese. This image of jolly service to the benevolent master unintentionally misleads us into the comfortable but false belief that farms are harmless, happy places.

The purpose of this book is to inform parents and children about factory-farm life—but it is incomplete. It has words and photographs, but it cannot let readers smell the stench of overcrowding and filth, it cannot let them hear the sounds of factory-farm violence and fear, and it cannot pass on the agony and despair of animals driven crazy by confinement and stress.

*At the moment our human world is based on the suffering and destruction of millions of non-humans. To perceive this and to begin to do something to change it in personal and public ways is to undergo a change in perception akin to religious or political conversion. Nothing can ever be seen in quite the same way again.*

Maureen Duffy, *Men and Beasts*

Bringing into the light the conditions of the factory farm and examining them with clear images will encourage us to become aware of what we are eating, to be alert to the vast cruelties of factory farming, to question our participation in this ugly process, and reawaken a sense of compassion for the animal kingdom. We must shake off the complacent images of farm animals and realize our bacon never basked in the sun, our eggs never nestled in straw-lined boxes and our veal never gambolled in green pastures. The pain of abused farm animals is the immediate and fundamental issue of this book. This is not a philosophical discussion on the interconnectedness of all life, nor a quest for the ideal relationship between man and animal, vegetarianism, nor even a criticism of centuries-old dining customs. Of course, with billions of animals now suffering in factory farms, these issues must be raised. But the purpose here is not to condemn the past, it is to help generate peace now between men and animals.

The miserable plight of factory animals is a simple concept and evokes simple compassion. And simple compassion is all it takes. The philosophy of caring and respect, which recognizes the interrelatedness of man and all other life forms on the planet, is growing—but it can still use all the help it can get. It is in this spirit that this book has come about. The callous factory-farming system will collapse of itself one day, when nobody will be party to its methods—thus ending the suffering of these animals.

> *. . . Why is compassion not part of our established curriculum, an inherent part of our education? Compassion, awe, wonder, curiosity, exaltation, humility—these are the very foundation of any real civilization, no longer the prerogatives, the preserves of any one church, but belonging to everyone, every child in every home, in every school.*
>
> Yehudi Menuhin, *Just for Animals*

> *The earth is the Lord's and the fullness thereof. Oh, God, enlarge within us the sense of fellowship with all living things, our brothers the animals to whom Thou gavest the earth as their home in common with us. We remember with shame that in the past we have exercised the high dominion of man with ruthless cruelty so that the voice of the earth, which should have gone up to Thee in song, has been a groan of travail. May we realise that they live not for us alone but for themselves and for Thee and that they love the sweetness of life.*
>
> St. Basil, Bishop of Caesarea
> 330–379 A.D.

2. A family of pigs together in a field is a rare sight; most US piglets are separated early from their mothers, and kept in confinement with others of the same age and size. The enforced company of their peers leads to fighting and social disorientation.

# 2

# Pigs

The traditional image of pigs rooting in the fields and wallowing in mud puddles is fast becoming little more than a memory. Practically speaking, piglets romping and squealing around the farmyard are only to be found in the illustrations of children's picture books.

This is because almost 90 percent of the roughly 85 million pigs slaughtered annually in the US spend most of their lives in close confinement, in overcrowded pens, in steel-barred crates, or in small multiple stacked cages, known as battery cages.

Since the 1950s, factory-farming techniques have been expanding in the industrialized world, and now are spreading to the Third World with money and technical assistance from international agribusiness. Hundreds of millions of pigs worldwide are now being raised intensively in conditions far more abusive and restrictive than the traditional pigsty.

## The Natural Pig

Pigs are known to be as intelligent as dogs; in fact, they have worked historically as hunting "dogs" and more recently as guard animals. They have been trained to race, pull carts, and do acrobatics, and they make loving, loyal, and clean companions—although adult pigs can take up a lot of space!

Pigs love to root in the ground for grubs and acorns with their powerful but sensitive snouts. In fact, in natural conditions, they spend up to six hours a day rooting around, grunting to each other and sniffing out buried tidbits. So acute is their sense of smell that pigs in France are taught to unearth truffles, a prized fungus and culinary delicacy which grows deep underground. In wartime, pigs have saved lives by detecting land mines buried out of sight.

Unfortunately, curses like "You filthy swine!" bolster the pigs' undeserved reputation for being dirty animals, yet given a choice pigs prefer being clean. If they have enough room, they naturally make separate areas for sleeping and defecating. Only when they are forced to live in close confinement do they foul their living area.

But they do like mud! Unlike humans, pigs have no sweat glands and are very sensitive to temperature. So to stay cool in hot weather and to rid their skin of parasites they need to roll in the dust—or better still, in nice goopy mud.

## The Factory Pig

Yet factory-raised pigs never have the freedom to roll in the mud, snuffle in the earth, or use their intelligence.

Factory-farm operators manipulate every aspect of the pig's life— from birth to death. Pigs are conceived, born, weaned, and fattened for slaughter in purpose-built buildings with automatic feeding, watering, manure removal, and environmental control equipment. In these conditions, however well-organized and modern they may be (and most animal factories, despite their modern equipment, are seldom clean and neat), pigs can never express their natural behavior patterns and never set foot on grass or even run outside.

Adult pigs normally grow to an average of 800 lbs (360 kg), although the record weight is over 1,900 lbs (860 kg). But factory-farm pigs, like most factory-farm animals, are killed before they even reach maturity. They are hauled off to the slaughterhouse as "teen-agers," at about 220 lbs (100 kg) and twenty-four weeks of age—at the rate of 250,000 per day.

*The breeding sow should be thought of as, and treated as, a valuable piece of machinery whose function is to pump out baby pigs like a sausage machine.*

L. J. Taylor, Export Development Manager,
Walls Meat Company Ltd.

## Behavior Patterns

The massed conditions of factory-farm life deny a pig's natural instincts and frustrate its normal activity, causing anxiety, social confusion—and the porcine equivalent of cultural boredom. The results are disturbed behavior patterns, some of which—because they damage the end product—the industry sees as "vices."

Tests show that young pigs cannot recognize more than thirty individuals in any group and they become deranged and aggressive when penned in large numbers. This is made worse by the practice of confining together animals of one age and sex, and not mixing them in more natural family patterns. Groups of mixed age and sex have built-in social mechanisms that prevent excessive aggressive behavior by any one subgroup.

In the crates and cages, extreme stress from understimulation is inevitable. Some of the resulting stereotypical "coping" behaviors are repetitive body movements, cage mouthing, bar gnawing, and sucking others' appendages and navels. But the major remedy for boredom—both in the pens and the cages—is to pick on each other, bite each other's tails and ears, and resort to what the industry calls "cannibalism."

The industry's cynical solution is to chop off the offending parts. Operators of pig factories, with their own strange logic, cut off the week-old piglet's tail—no anesthetics—to prevent it being chewed off a couple of months later by bored cage mates.

More mutilations are performed on the week-old piglet: eight teeth are clipped off with wire cutters; identification notches are cut into the ear; and males have their testicles cut off—again no anesthetics—to reduce their aggression in crowded areas (this is also justified by the claim that uncastrated boar meat has an unpleasant taste).

Producers also use environmental controls to limit these behavioral problems—problems *caused* essentially by their inhumane husbandry practices. Lights, for example, are turned off or dimmed in hog barns except at feeding time to reduce excited behavior; researchers report that pigs kept in the dark sit for long periods in a depressed, mournful attitude. Factory pigs may never see the light of day until they are on their way to auction or slaughter.

Clearly, pigs' aggressive and abnormal behavior results from early weaning and is the inevitable reaction to social confusion, inactivity, confinement, overcrowding, and the almost-complete suppression of natural behavior. Abusive methods of control cannot eliminate behavioral problems when pigs are denied their every natural instinct and need. Attempts to fit pigs into the factory-farm system and to mold the perfect pork animal say more about the arrogant stupidity of man than the deficiencies of pigs.

# Breeding: Factory Style

A factory breeding sow averages 2 1/2 litters a year, and 10 litters in a lifetime. With ten or eleven piglets per litter, she brings 100–110 piglets into the system during the first four to five years of her life. After this exhausting period, she is no longer cost-effective and is slaughtered.

To be efficient as a reproductive unit, the sow must produce the maximum number of live piglets in the shortest time. By force-weaning piglets at an unnaturally early age, operators can reimpregnate the sow sooner and accelerate the normal reproductive cycle. No regard is paid for the distress and suffering caused by these continual pregnancies, separations, and frustrated maternal instincts.

When weaning takes place depends on the economics of the piglets' survival rate. The earlier they are weaned, the sooner the sow can be reimpregnated—but many piglets will probably die. If they are weaned later, more piglets will survive—but the operator may not be getting the most out of his sow, for she is at her most efficient when she is pregnant.

When she is not pregnant—or at least nursing—she is wasting resources, and the feed and housing costs of this unproductive downtime between pregnancies must be minimized. So the operator strives to ensure the earliest reimpregnation. Since a sow may be fertile for only a very short period of time during her cycle, operators use a variety of methods not to miss the occasion, and to keep the sow relentlessly productive.

Sometimes a boar is let loose among the tethered sows, the so-called rape rack, but most larger operators consider artificial insemination a more efficient method of controlling the reproductive process. This permits the selection of "desirable" genetic traits, such as faster weight gain and meatier bodies.

Other operators use inferior boars to sniff out and stimulate sows at the peak of their cycles, then repeatedly frustrate them from completing the job; actual insemination is performed, not by the boar, but artificially by the operator or a veterinarian. Some sniffer boars are known as "sidewinders" because they have had their penises surgically rerouted to exit at the side.

Aerosol spray cans of artificial aphrodisiacs (synthetic hormones similar to a boar's natural odor) are sometimes used to speed up the heat period and stimulate the sow, thus improving the chances of fertilization by artificial insemination.

Another method of impregnation involves the surgical transplant of embryos from "supersows" to ordinary sows. The ovaries of sows with

3. Old MacDonald's lucky piglets are enjoying the sun with their mother while their father looks happily on. Of the roughly 80 million pigs slaughtered in the US each year, only a handful will grow up and live like this in the relative freedom of the old-fashioned pig sty.

the desired genetic traits are stimulated with drugs to release a large number of eggs at one time. The eggs are then artificially fertilized with the semen from a genetically suitable boar. Later, an embryotomy is performed; the embryos are surgically removed from the sow. Such a productive "supersow" must endure being cut open and sewn back up several times a year.

The boar and the "supersows" may live hundreds of miles apart and the embryos may be implanted in sows in still different locations. This highly invasive technique typifies the industry's callous approach to all animal reproduction and to what it considers the genetic uncertainties of natural procreation—and symbolizes its inhumane, commercial, and technological view of the value of animal life.

Pigs are selectively bred for commercial advantages. Resistance to disease, leanness, and body length are the sought-after traits, not their natural qualities, like mothering for example. Indeed, genetic manipulation commonly results in poor mothers and higher piglet mortality. Researchers in the US report that on the factory farm, up to 18 percent of piglets are crushed to death by the mother.

Additionally, according to the Meat and Livestock Commission in Great Britain, 2–5 percent of piglets are born with congenital defects such as splayed legs, hermaphrodism, no anus, inverted teats, and hernias. That represents some 500,000 deformed piglets a year in the UK.

4. This is not a steel tubing factory; it's home for hundreds of pregnant sows. In row upon row of individual gestation crates, sows spend three months, three weeks, and three days of torturous boredom and inactivity, awaiting the birth of their piglets. They have neither straw nor other bedding—only bare boards and hard concrete. They cannot turn around, they never go outside—and there's no relief.

## The Gestation Period

Once pregnant, the life of the young breeding sow is bleak, rigid, and unvaried. While she awaits delivery of her piglets, like millions of other pregnant sows in the US, she is confined in a steel-barred cage, called a gestation crate, for about three months and three weeks without interruption.

A gestation crate typically measures two feet by six feet (60 cm × 182 cm). The floors are either of steel mesh, concrete, or slats, or a combination. No straw or bedding is provided. In the crate the sow can move neither forward nor backward nor turn around. She may also be chained to her stall or chained by the waist to the floor.

The gestation crate effectively prevents all physical activity, and although the cages are set in rows, the breeding sow cannot interact socially with the other pigs around her. Certainly, her solitary confinement is a far cry from the free and natural environments pigs enjoy in children's books.

With nothing to look forward to and no activity permitted by the confinement of the crate, eating is the only pleasure. Unfortunately for these omnivores who naturally eat a wide range of foods—and who have twice as many taste buds as humans—it is the same monotonous, medicated food day after day.

Even this one highlight of the day may be denied; many operators "skip-feed" their gestating and farrowing sows, feeding them only every other day, or even less often than that. They claim the sows get too fat—an obvious consequence of never getting any exercise.

A sow's natural tendency to keep separate areas for sleeping and defecating is denied in the crate. She must lie in her own mess and can get rid of it only by forcing it through the slatted or steel mesh floor with the weight of her body.

*If a man aspires to a righteous life, his first act of abstinence is from injury to animals.*

Count Leo Tolstoy, *The First Step*

Sows fight wildly against the confinement when first introduced to the gestation crate, especially if they are chained. They often fight for days, until beaten by the system. Frequently, this vain struggle results in sores and serious injuries—and who can tell what psychological pain is inflicted on this animal which we know is at least as intelligent as the family dog?

Perhaps the sight of gestating sows standing motionless in orthostatic shock, or swaying their bodies and heads back and forth all day, or mouthing and gnawing on the cage bars tells some of the story. According to research in Holland, these repetitive movements, or stereotypes, are "coping behaviors"—indicators of psychological disturbance instinctively developed to deal with the stress of understimulation and confinement. Similar rhythmic, trancelike movements are often seen in caged zoo animals. A report from the Scottish Farm Buildings Investigation Unit in the UK notes that the way in which sows adapt to close confinement resembles the *human* development of chronic, psychiatric disorders.

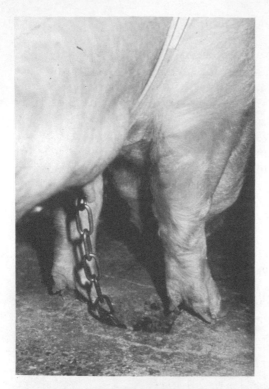

5. If we chained a dog on such a short leash for over three months with no break, we would rightly be accused of gross cruelty. Is it any less cruel to chain up a pig?

6. "Mouthing" the bars of the crate is an unnatural behavior pattern—the industry calls it a "vice"—which helps confined pigs cope with the stress and boredom of deprivation and inactivity.

# Farrowing

In natural surroundings, in the field, or in housing with enough freedom of movement, the nurturing mother pig prepares for the birth of her young by building a nest of grass, leaves, or straw. When the piglets are born, she lies with them in the nest, keeps them warm and carefully avoids squashing them.

But when the factory sow is ready to give birth—or farrow—she is moved from one barren steel cage to another, from the gestation crate to the farrowing crate. Given no bedding, no straw, and no room to move, she is frustrated and distracted at being unable to make a nest for her piglets, and completely loses her mothering skills. She becomes clumsy with her little ones, sometimes crushes them when she sits or rolls over—and, disoriented by her confinement, may occasionally eat one. (Some vets advise pig breeders to grind up dead piglets, the afterbirth and any deformed newborns, and feed them back to the sows.) She cannot even keep them warm on the slatted concrete or steel floors. With no straw and no bedding, the piglets are deprived from the most simple comfort of nestling with their mother; in cold weather they must huddle away from her under a heat lamp.

The pregnant sow stays in the farrowing crate from a few days before giving birth until her piglets are weaned. After farrowing, she is commonly strapped to the floor with a leather band, or held down in a lying position by steel bars, to keep her teats continuously exposed. Her piglets are thus encouraged to suckle at any time, promoting their most rapid growth possible. But the sow, unable to stand up, is allowed no respite from their constant attention.

The factory-farm process destroys the sow's progression of instinctual behavior and deprives her of the ability to fulfill her natural birthing rituals. Swedish and Scottish researchers have noted that mouthing, rooting, and nosing the bars and cage floor, longer birthing times, and higher rates of piglet mortality are evidence of the caged sow's frustrated mothering instincts. The same researchers also remarked that these symptoms of stress disappear when the sow is given a stall with straw where she can build a nest and farrow in comfort.

The sow's body is treated like a piece of machinery. It is impregnated without her consent or participation—natural mating behavior between boar and sow is often denied. The sow is then cruelly kept in a kind of suspended animation, squeezed into a steel crate for the duration of her pregnancy so that she never enjoys the freedom of farmyard or green grassy fields. Next she is moved to a different steel crate where the babies are born—no nesting is allowed here. This

7. Old MacDonald's sow stretches out with her brood on a nest she made of straw—but in the barren farrowing crate, this nesting ritual is denied. Straw is too much trouble for the operators and too much money. Scientists know that symptoms of this frustration—mouthing the bars, rooting and nosing the cage floor, longer birth times, and higher piglet mortality—disappear when nesting material is given.

farrowing crate, in which she cannot turn around, is too small to allow mothering care for her young. Her body is strapped down and becomes a perpetual soda fountain. She never has the freedom to take a break from the constant sucking, to stand up, shake off her piglets, and walk away from them, like "free range" animals or human mothers. Finally, the function of feeding her offspring is broken off by forced early weaning; and any remaining maternal bonding or satisfaction from nurturing her piglets is prematurely shattered. Mothering instincts and psychological needs, already dulled by generations of genetic manipulation and months in the gestation crate, are completely crushed and frustrated by the physical constraints and economic policies of agribusiness.

8. Trapped in her steel cage, the sow's nipples are always available to her piglets, so they can gain weight fast and be weaned early. When the piglets are newly born, the mother is sometimes strapped down at the neck so she cannot rise. The heat lamp (at bottom left) keeps the piglets warm in cooler weather, because they have no nest to share with their mother.

## A Piglet's Life

Piglets wean themselves naturally at eight to twelve weeks of age; in the factory farm, they are force-weaned at three weeks or sooner. Many early-weaned piglets die; the earlier they are weaned, the fewer survive. Not surprisingly, scientists report early separation from their mothers leads later to abnormal behavior, including sucking the bellies and appendages of other pigs.

Newly weaned piglets are placed in cages with mechanical feeding and watering systems, where the operator can theoretically control temperature, lighting, atmosphere, and diet. These cages, stacked in rows, are called battery cages and allow the operator to raise many more pigs per square foot of building area than possible in ground level pens.

A typical battery cage measures about 3'9" × 3'9" (115 cm × 115 cm) and is made of heavy wire with wire mesh floors. Eight piglets are crammed into each one. A piglet has only 1 3/4 square feet of space

(1/6 sq m or 1,626 sq cm) to itself. In 1981 in the US, 26 million piglets spent their early months is stacked nursery cages or in similar confinement.

There is no running around the farmyard for these young animals; conditions in the cages prohibit piglets' natural playfulness and normal social behavior. With their cloven feet, they have difficulty standing on wire mesh—and romping about the cage can result in severe foot and leg injuries. Most of the time they stay lying down, keeping the weight off their feet; and their legs become weak and susceptible to lameness.

Other piglets are packed into large pens with up to seventy-five others, and like their caged cousins, they have less than two square feet (1/5 sq m) of living space each (for comparison, a record album cover is almost exactly one square foot). As they grow older, the numbers of pigs per cage are reduced but because the pigs are now larger in size, there is little relief from the crush.

*The pig . . . is a naturally active, intelligent and above all inquisitive animal with a strong inclination to explore and root about.*

Report of the Agricultural Committee,
the House of Commons, United Kingdom, 1981

## Disease and Drugs

Animals in their natural state suffer from disease, but the factory farm concentrates and magnifies such problems, and adds many of its own. Although one worker can handle over five hundred pigs in a totally controlled system, conditions rule out the individual attention sick animals need.

Pigs in confinement suffer from a number of diseases directly related to the conditions in which they live and made worse by the pressure of the factory environment. Among these are problems with bone development, such as necrosis of the back muscles, sometimes called "banana disease" because stricken pigs arch their backs into a banana shape; "bacteria buildup" in factory-farm buildings because they are used year round without adequate cleaning; porcine stress syndrome (PSS), or malignant hyperthermia; and psychological problems caused both by overcrowding and prevention of natural behavior patterns and by understimulation and boredom in environments alien to a pig's instinctive needs.

9. Life is no picnic for the millions of newly weaned piglets who are crammed six or eight to a cage in stacked battery rows. With their cloven feet, they risk injury on the wire mesh floors if they scamper about in play. Over 50 percent of factory pigs are lame when slaughtered.

10. The steel mesh floors of some stacked cages allow a constant shower of feces and urine from the upper cages to fall on those below. Forced rapid growth and intensive feeding in factory farms are another cause of lameness in pigs whose bodies are genetically engineered for meatiness, not for the sturdiness of their legs.

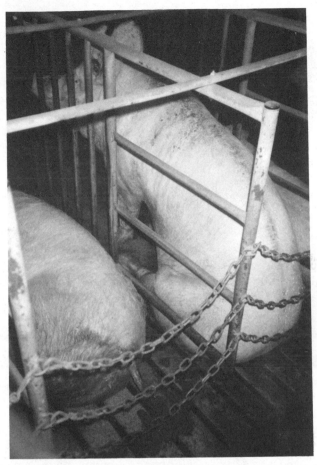

11. Lights are often turned off or dimmed in hog barns—except at feeding times for the handlers' convenience. Researchers report that pigs kept in the dark sit for long periods in a depressed mournful attitude—like this gestating (pregnant) sow.

In these confinement systems, the high levels of dust and the concentration of ammonia and other fumes from the manure and urine are overpowering. This health hazard, together with lack of exercise, results in 35–60 percent of all confined pigs suffering from respiratory disease. Pity also the piglets in the lower rows of battery cages; they are bombarded from above by the droppings and urine falling through the mesh floors of the upper cages.

Pigs confined in crates and cages frequently suffer injuries to their legs. Neither steel mesh nor metal slatted flooring is an appropriate or comfortable surface for cloven feet. This factor, together with the industry's trend of breeding for faster growing, meatier bodies while at the same time disregarding the need for commensurately stronger legs, results in over 50 percent of all pigs being lame at the time of slaughter.

Producers try to promote faster growth and resolve disease problems—present or anticipated—by constantly and indiscriminately dosing pigs with antibiotics and other legally permitted drugs and medications (twelve thousand are legally permitted in the US). Drug residues in the meat are the inevitable result of pigs' lifelong ingestion of food additives, with the attendant risks of continuous low dosage of these drugs for the human consumers of factory meat.

# Conclusion

Astonishingly, the factory-farming industry claims that its controlled systems are better for the animals than natural environments. Parasites, disease, and predators are all cited as good reasons for protecting the "poor animals" from the dangers of the open field and moving them into the cozy factory-farm system. Modern farm animals raised in confinement, it is also alleged, "have adapted to this type of agriculture and could not survive well in a barnyard or range environment." And yet the evidence shows the instinctual needs and behavioral patterns of animals are blunted by confinement, but not erased. When released from the constraints of the factory farm, animals soon return to their "natural" behavior.

Confined animals are made to suffer greatly in exchange for the dubious safety of the man-made environment, even though they are assured of a constant supply of water and food—albeit mixed with antibiotics, drugs, and other additives. Confinement in small cages, overcrowding, physical stress and injury, mutilation, and gross psychological deprivation are the inhumane price which the animals are forced to pay. Despite industry claims of better care, would animals be willing to pay this price if they had a choice? One experiment in England suggests not; 100 percent of chickens given the choice between nesting in the cage or the open field, chose the open field.

Most people acknowledge that wild animals have a basic right to their natural habitats, not because the animals serve any economic purpose but simply because they are wild and part of our global heritage. Indeed, millions of dollars are spent annually by government and conservation organizations to preserve environments for such wildlife.

Though no longer wild, pigs are also animals—but they receive very different treatment. For most people, they are merely farm animals whose only reason for existence is the bacon in "bacon and eggs." Yet, like every other creature on the planet, pigs exist for their own purposes, whether we humans can perceive those purposes or not. Pigs are not the exclusive, exploitable property of our species and, even though humans are at present unable to see more than food value in a pig's existence, they surely deserve more compassionate treatment at the hands of today's pork producers than they are currently receiving. We certainly should not be fooled—by our memories of farms and by the idealized pictures in children's books—into thinking a pig's life is all in clover.

12. This is the farm of our childhood. The sun shines down. Contented animals graze on fresh green grass. The clear stream flows by. Crops, orchards, pastures, and garden plot are all integrated elements in the old-fashioned farm ideal—people, animals, and earth in harmony. We grew up thinking this is where food comes from. But, however idyllic the traditional country picture may appear, it is virtually impossible to use animals for our own ends without condemning them to grossly unnatural lives, often involving much cruelty and suffering.

# 3

# Dairy Cows

In 1989, there were just over 10 million dairy cows in the US living on fewer than 300,000 farms. Although there are only half as many cows now as there were thirty years ago, there are also literally millions fewer farms now than then. This means that the average herd size has increased dramatically. Dairy herds of several hundred cows are now common.

But these larger numbers mean mass-production methods of animal handling and impersonal, distant treatment. Individual care and attention—essentials to the welfare of the dairy cow—are an amenity that the dairy producer cannot afford in time or money. Poor "Ole Bessie," whose every idiosyncrasy the traditional small farmer knew so well, is now no more than a series of statistics with a number stapled to her ear.

> *There can be no doubt in the mind of every thinking man that the concept of dominion as expressed in the Torah . . . does not imply the rule of a despot. . . . Heaven forfend that such a repulsive form of servitude be forever sealed into the world of the Lord, Whose tender mercies are in all his works.*
>
> Rabbi Kuk

The sole reason a cow makes milk is to feed her own calf. Like all mammal mothers, including humans, she suckles her young from the time it is born until its body can handle regular food. In nature, the

49

milk flows only as long as the calf suckles. As the growing calf satisfies its increasing biological need for grass and roughage, it nurses less and less and the mother's milk supply then tapers off, eventually drying up.

But long ago men developed a taste for cow's milk and found they could keep the milk flowing by pulling and squeezing the cow's teats by hand, imitating the calf's sucking action. So for centuries, farmers shared the milk with the calf until it was old enough to eat grass and hay. They also fed it leftover dairy by-products like skim milk and whey. Then, when the calf was weaned, they kept all the milk for themselves.

Today, dairy operators do not share any cow's milk with the newborn and young calves. In fact, calves are commonly taken away from their mothers as early as the day they are born. Often, they are not even allowed the colostrum, the natural antibiotic complex needed for good health, which mammal mothers—including humans—produce in the first milk they give their young.

Some female calves are kept for future milking but the surplus females and most male calves are sent to auction, to the profitable, but ugly veal business. The dairy operator generally has no use for the newborn calf; for him, it is no more than the trigger that starts the milk—and money—flowing.

We know that a calf naturally suckles about twenty times a day, and in like manner, the cow's body is designed to be milked a little and often. This means that in nature the cow is never burdened with carrying large quantities of milk.

In contrast, modern high-yielding cows must retain their extra-heavy loads of milk in their bodies for long periods of time. Huge, deformed udders are common in dairy herds today, udders so distended they scrape the ground or are kicked and scratched by the cow's own rear hooves. No wonder cows always seem so helpful at milking time and stand ready in line—they can't wait to be relieved of their painful load. As any nursing human mother knows, overfull breasts cause great discomfort.

The cow normally "dries up" after ten months or so, but during her lactation period she has no voluntary control over the quantity of milk she produces. Through a natural metabolic process, she produces milk more or less in proportion to the amount removed.

Taking advantage of this natural metabolic process, dairy operators have pushed milk flow to its limits. They do not concern themselves too much with the long-term health of the cow, nor with the debilitating physical effects this overloading of her natural systems will have on

13. Phyllis, Agatha, and Toby wait while Old MacDonald milks Sue Anne. Donkeys and dogs, cats and geese, chickens and lots of wild piglets romp around this happy harmonious farmyard—this is the image we absorb as children and it insulates us from the harsh realities of the factory farm.

her. Rather than maintain the cow in good health for a full fifteen- to twenty-year lifetime, it is easier and cheaper to "milk" her for all she is worth, keeping her going on stimulants and drugs—and then replace her after a few years when she "wears out."

While her calf is nursing, the cow can easily replace what it drinks; but when the farmer pumps her dry with his sophisticated vacuum milking machine, her body must strain to replace the large quantity taken. The cow is sucked dry twice, sometimes three times a day—it only takes ten minutes. Meanwhile, her body labors; and the unrelenting milking machine, together with the special feeds and drugs, artificially prolongs her natural milk cycle. During this lactation period she must produce ten times more milk for the farmers' insatiable mechanical "calf" than her own calf would have drunk if left to suckle its full term.

## Feedlot Dairies

Factory cows sadly do not graze in the lush rolling meadows of picture books; indeed, for these cows there are no green meadows except those they may glimpse over the fence.

Increasingly dairy factory operations are being located near large

14. These high-yielding dairy cows are sucked dry two, and sometimes three times a day in high-tech milk factories still quaintly called "milking parlors." No Phyllis, Agatha, or Toby here—only numbered ear-tags. The only interaction between the cow and her keeper standing at udder height on the lower floor is when he attaches the milking machine.

centers of population to reduce transport costs; the milk is closer to the consumers and the cows are nearer to the feedstuff suppliers. Land costs are higher but then not much land is used.

Cows on feedlot dairies never go out to pasture; they are confined continuously in closed barns or open-air pens that they never leave—except to walk a few feet to adjacent milking parlors. These holding areas permit the operator to monitor and manipulate the unnaturally rich mix of high-energy grains and grain by-products, silage, and hay required to force the high milk yield.

Outdoor yards are usually no more than feedlot-style pens with little shade or shelter—a dustbowl in summer, deep mud in winter. In grassy pastures, cows like to spend up to twelve hours a day lying down but these pens offer no clean, comfortable resting places. Cows must lie in their own feces in the dirt, mud, or concrete; many get mastitis, a painful udder infection, from the constant filth.

Indoor holding sheds are no better—and have little in common with

Old MacDonald's cozy, straw-filled barn where his animals snuggled in winter. Surrounded by concrete and steel, the crowded cows hang about the feed source, year in, year out, wading in ankle-deep excrement. They may only find relief from the slimy concrete floors—some cows wear holes in their hooves on the hard, rough surface—in raised resting places where they can lie down, separated from one another by steel bars.

But these are the lucky ones; some operators keep their cows chained at the neck in narrow stalls, often for many months at a time during winter. These poor milk machines can only eat, lactate, and defecate. They can neither turn around, groom themselves, nor scratch an itch.

In any herd, one cow emerges as the leader. The others develop a social order, with low-ranking cows giving way to higher-ranking ones. This behavior pattern may seem undemocratic to us, but in ancestral days, the established leader helped the herd to function as a cooperative unit while feeding and protecting itself. Domesticated cows still need this ranking mechanism to find their niche in the herd and retain individual identities. The traditional farmer appreciated this hierarchy; he depended on his lead cow, or "Bossie," to bring in the herd from the fields at milking time.

Conditions in factory dairy farms thwart these natural behavioral needs and create psychological stress among the ranks. Where too many cows are penned in too little space, this ranking order is difficult to establish and maintain. Junior and submissive cows, unable to keep their distance, unavoidably violate the space of their social superiors, and suffer the consequences; they are upset while ruminating, turned out of their resting places by senior cows, and bullied away from the food before getting enough to eat.

We should remember that the barn, the yard, and the stall are not just workplaces where these "zero grazed" cows pass a few hours each day; they spend their whole lives cooped up in these conditions—eating and waiting. Operators may save the labor, expense, and inconvenience of herding cows to and from fields at milking time, but can this incarceration be justified on any grounds other than economic? The imprisoned cows never graze naturally in open pastures, never enjoy the shelter and shade of trees, and never lie down and chew the cud in comfort. Modern factory dairy cows never see a fresh blade of grass from birth to death.

Thirty years ago, the average cow produced 2.5 tons of milk a year; today, after many generations of selective breeding and programs of intensive nutrition, she produces nearly 7 tons a year; and still the industry searches for new means of raising her productivity.

15. Inside a typical dairy barn—concrete floors, steel stalls, and thick excrement everywhere. These dairy cows move endlessly to-and-fro between the barn and the "milking parlor." They never graze outside. If they ever see a green grassy field, it's through the barn doors or from the truck on the way to slaughter.

*It should not be believed that all beings exist for the sake of the existence of man. On the contrary, all other beings too have been intended for their own sakes and not for the sake of anything else.*

Maimonides (Rabbi Moses ben Maimon)

Veterinary scientists know that this superproductive, overworked cow is not the placid gentle creature we recall from nursery tales. She is a highly stressed animal; indeed, one British scientist has described the work done by a dairy cow in peak lactation as equivalent to "a human being jogging six hours every day." The industry's heavy demands on her body have made her more prone than her ancestors to disease. Among her health problems are serious metabolic disorders such as ketosis, where the cow breaks down her own body tissue to produce milk, leading to weight loss, infertility and general ill health; chronic catarrh; digestive diseases such as rumen acidosis and associated laminitis, a painful hoof condition; and many more, including udder complaints like mastitis. Every year in Britain, one-third of the dairy herd is treated for mastitis with teat sprays and intramammary injections of antibiotics—some of which are also used to treat humans.

Then in 1986, a "wonder drug," bovine somatotrophin (a naturally occurring but artificially boosted bovine growth hormone), became available. Known as BST or bGH, this controversial drug increases milk flow by up to 40 percent from these already-overstretched cows. Now pity the poor "wonder drugged" dairy cow, fed food too rich for her health, never grazing, standing in a barn or yard all her life, milked three times a day, producing nearly 8.5 tons of milk a year, or nearly seven gallons a day—and receiving her daily "fix" by injection. She may be an efficient biological machine, but at what cost to her real welfare? Because this "pin cushion cow" needs more concentrated foods, she is more susceptible to lameness and rumen disorders. She is even more liable to infectious and contagious diseases, she may have problems calving, and the physiological stress of producing so much milk will cause her to burn out sooner, in as few as three years.

Cows naturally live for close to twenty years, but very few, if any, ever die of natural causes in their old age. By the time the regular modern milking cow is six to seven years old, she has been worn out. She has been artificially inseminated four to five times, has had four to five calves taken away from her in the first few days after birth, and has produced about twenty-five to thirty tons of milk. When her milk production slows down, this no longer efficient unit of agricultural output is sent off to slaughter. Her body, not yet old, but already too tough for the prime cuts of beef, is usually ground into hamburger— and ends up on a sesame bun with ketchup, relish, and, ironically, cheese.

The storybook cow is limpid-eyed, cozy and motherly, nursing her calf and grazing in pleasant green pastures, her horns uplifted, perhaps a bell hanging round her neck. Sadly this image is a far cry from the reality of the long-suffering factory cow. Dairy industry literature and children's books keep telling us how cows like to "give" us their milk—but we should realize that in truth, the milk is not given, it is taken by force; extracted as efficiently as possible from a grossly exploited animal.

*The greatness of a nation and its moral progress can be judged by the way its animals are treated.*

Mohandas Gandhi,
*The Moral Basis of Vegetarianism*

# Reproduction

Dairy cows must be artificially impregnated once a year to keep up milk production, and usually give birth to just one calf—a young cow usually has her first calf at age two. A cow who fails to produce a calf cannot produce milk and is soon sent off to slaughter.

Certain cows, however, selected for their superior genetic characteristics, are used for mass-production breeding—in similar manner to the "supersows" mentioned in the chapter on pigs. These "supercows" may be forced to produce up to eighty calves a year—yes, eighty.

This is how. The "supercow" is dosed with hormones that stimulate the ovaries to release many eggs, instead of the normal one or two. Drugs may be used to bring her in heat on demand. When in heat, she is impregnated artificially with semen from a "superbull"—one who has already proven high-yielding offspring—and her eggs are fertilized. Just days later, the embryos are flushed out of the "supercow" with sterile water.

After sorting by sex, the unwanted embryos are discarded; the rest are surgically implanted into ordinary cows. These animals need not all be on the same farm; in fact, semen and embryos are sent all over the world. Embryos implanted in Australian dairy cows may come from a Pennsylvania "supercow" with semen collected from a "superbull" in France.

After a 280-day gestation period, a calf is born. Unfortunately, surrogate cows sometimes have difficulty giving birth normally, as the implanted calf may be larger than one she would naturally bear. The dairyman's solution is painful to both cow and calf; he attaches a chain to the calf's forelegs and winches it out.

Mother and calf recognize each other by smell and voice, and the bonding between them is strong. In natural surroundings the calf runs alongside its mother within hours of birth, and, as we have seen, may take a year to wean itself fully.

The dairy operator however breaks this relationship by removing the calf a few days after birth, usually within twenty-four hours. The prolonged cries of anguish of both mother and calf are heartrending, as anyone who has heard will tell. They will not see each other again. This trauma of losing her calf happens once a year for the cow.

*If you have men who will exclude any of God's creatures from the shelter of compassion and pity, you will have men who will deal likewise with their fellow men.*

St. Francis of Assisi

## Conclusion

While factory-farm animals raised for food live short lives, it could be said that their suffering, though intense, is also short. Dairy cows live foreshortened lives too, but they are burdened with even greater daily abuse than their cousins, the beef cattle. Not only must they endure close confinement and all that that entails, but these animals are made to work continuously to the limits of their capacities, capacities which have been unnaturally stretched by excessively high protein diets, drugs and hormones, and the mass-production methods of the operators.

Sometimes we drive our cars without heed for long-term maintenance; indeed, we may wear them out and run them into the ground. But have we the right to do the same to living, sentient beings? Society thinks of dairy foods as the willing offerings of live animals who lead pleasant country lives and remain unharmed by the experience of

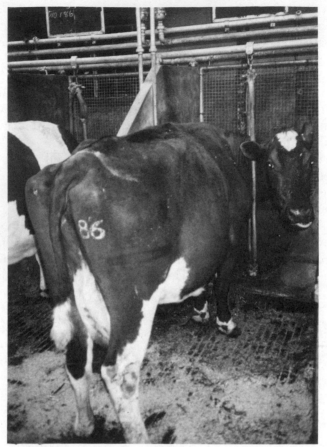

16. We should remember that the stall, the barn, and the yard are not just workplaces where these "zero-grazed" cows spend a few hours each day; they live their whole lives cooped up in these conditions—eating and waiting.

"giving" us their milk. Indeed, milk products have all the aura of motherhood and nurturing, of goodness and health, of soft, gentle, rural life. But the wrench of mother/calf separation, the killing of the unwanted calves, the endless grind of the barn or holding pen, and the premature slaughter of the cow herself are parts of this equation which we conveniently overlook.

Can we justify our huge consumption of dairy products when these animals are suffering to such an extent? Although the animal from which the milk is taken may be alive at the time of milking, pain and death are always present. The modern dairy cow is the classic case of an animal who is misused, abused, and then tossed out. Every pound of butter embodies her daily ordeal, and in every glass of milk flits the shadow of her calf.

17. Dimly-lit veal barns like this sometimes hold hundreds of calves, each in its individual narrow crate. There's no gambolling or frolicking here; just one step forward, one step back, no turning around, no grooming, and barely enough room to lie down.

# 4

# Veal Calves

While modern high-tech farming sees animals as units of economic input which must operate at peak efficiency—or be killed, children's books show calves gamboling in green pastures with their mothers, smelling the flowers and enjoying the fresh air and sunshine. This may be the life for beef calves out on the range, but for most dairy calves, it's another, harsher story.

Separated from their mothers, male and female dairy calves are shut up in small crates or pens. Most are destined to be killed for veal. For these calves there is no room to gambol, there are no green pastures, and there are no flowers. Some of the females are kept alive to replace their mothers when they are worn out by the strains of factory dairy production. To keep the operators' costs down, future milking cows commonly spend their adolescence crowded into small feedlot-style dirt pens, awaiting impregnation and their first lactation cycle.

Traditionally, the source of veal was quick and simple; beef calves and unwanted dairy calves—the male "bobbies" and surplus females—were slaughtered soon after birth. But today in the US, while many male dairy calves are raised for beef, roughly one million calves a year, more than 30 percent of US veal production, are raised for premium "milk fed veal."

The meat industry considers premium "milk fed" veal to be a status item. In fact, it is the product of an especially cruel and restrictive confinement system. This system, first developed in Holland, is simple to operate and shows quick profits, which is why it has spread worldwide over the last thirty years.

Three factors have led to this speedy growth: the constant supply of unwanted calves from the dairy industry; the availability of cheap dairy by-products to feed them; and the willingness of gastronomes to pay high prices for this "sought after" meat.

> *An animal should have at least sufficient freedom of movement to be able without difficulty, to turn around, groom itself, get up, lie down and stretch its limbs.*

Brambell Report to the British Parliament, on Farm
Animal Welfare, 1965

## The System

The concept is simple yet very cruel; from birth, calves are kept in solitary confinement in small wooden crates, deprived of mobility, iron, and fiber in their food. This keeps their flesh the desired pale color. At four months or less they are slaughtered, and the veal producer makes a handsome profit because the system has greatly increased the amount of salable pale meat per animal.

But after four months of physical and psychological deprivation the calves are sick animals; they cannot be kept longer because too many would die. As it is, up to 20 percent of calves in veal crates die of disease and stress—and heartbreak—before slaughter age. As one British veterinary scientist put it, "The calf born to the dairy cow is routinely submitted to more insults to normal development than any other farm animal."

Although the veal crate system is more "efficient" at producing more pale meat per animal, such high productivity—and the high profits of the veal growers—totally ignores the agony of the young calves' lives. But as long as consumers demand this anemic, not particularly nutritious meat, this especially abusive sector of factory farming will probably continue to exist. In England, however, the veal crate has been outlawed as a result of public pressure.

## The Veal Crate

The average veal crate is made of wood and measures 22" wide by 54" long (56 cm × 137 cm); that is just enough space for a calf to stand or lie down, but not to turn around. Virtually all physical activity is deliberately prevented; exercise would increase muscle development, toughen the meat, and slow weight gain.

Some crates hold the calf's head permanently between two vertical wooden slats, which permit only up or down movement. More often the calf is chained by the neck allowing only one step forward or one step back.

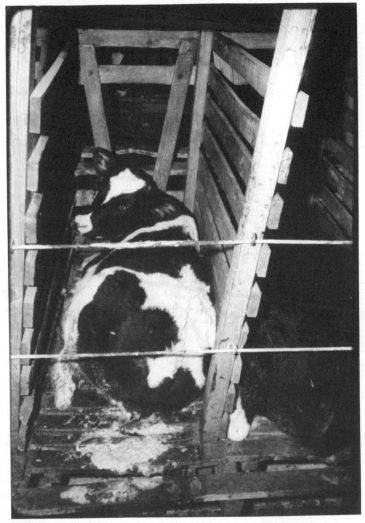

18. A calf raised for veal spends its whole life—sixteen weeks—in solitary confinement in a crate like this, too narrow for it even to turn around and groom itself. A children's coloring book from the Wisconsin Agri-Business Foundation describes the bare wooden crate as "somewhat like the crib you had when you were a baby."

Unable to turn around, the calf cannot groom or lick itself properly. It cannot lie down in a natural, comfortable position, nor can it stretch out its legs. By the time a calf is 350 pounds and ready for slaughter, even lying down may be impossible in the narrow crate.

Wooden veal crates have slatted or barred floors, designed to allow the calf's droppings to pass through. However, the constant strain of standing on this insecure footing usually leads to painfully swollen knee joints. Additionally, the calves' improper diet brings on diarrhea—called scours—which makes the slats slippery and wet, causing falls and leg injuries. For these reasons—and from total lack of exercise—most crated veal calves can hardly walk when taken off to slaughter.

Calves are given no straw or bedding in the crates, because this would clog up the manure disposal system and involve added labor and expense for the producer. Calves live and sleep on the bare slats. Incredibly and very deceptively, a Wisconsin agribusiness coloring book aimed at children describes the veal crate as being "somewhat like the crib you had when you were a baby"!

## A Calf's Diet: No Iron, No Fiber, No Water

A cow's first milk after giving birth is called colostrum. Human babies—and other mammals—also receive colostrum from their mothers during the first days of nursing. This special substance gives protection against disease in the form of natural antibodies and natural antibiotics. Depending on the individual dairy farmer's whim—or on when the truck is coming to take the calves away—some calves receive the colostrum from their mothers before they are separated; others are taken away at birth and do not get the benefit of it.

A calf naturally nurses and runs with its mother—if permitted to do so—for nearly a year. In the first few weeks it suckles about twenty times a day, then gradually weans itself as it begins to include grass and roughage in its diet.

But the crated veal calf receives only a large bucketful of liquid feed twice a day. This psychologically and physically stressful factory-feeding regime—in line with the other elements of the confinement system—completely ignores the young mammal's natural need to suckle from its mother a little but often.

Whether forcibly weaned at a day or a week, a young calf does not lose this strong biological urge to suckle and its denial causes great frustration. A crated calf will suck pathetically on anything it can reach.

The veal calf is fed a liquid "milk replacer"; a mix of growth stimulators, powdered skim milk, starch, fats, sugar, vitamins, mold inhibitors, and antibiotics—so the "milk fed" description of this veal is really a misnomer. This mixture is designed to keep the flesh pale, to speed weight gain, and to keep the animal just healthy enough to survive until slaughtered.

Crated calves are allowed no drinking water. Temperatures are often kept high in the barns so that in a futile attempt to quench its thirst, the calf will consume large quantities of the liquid diet and put on weight fast.

The calf's flesh is kept pale by restricting the intake of dietary iron, since this contributes to the red color of meat. The calf is born with stores of iron in its body, but by eight to ten weeks this is used up. With no iron the calf would die; so the amount of iron in the diet is strictly controlled to keep the calf alive—but chronically anemic.

A calf starts to crave roughage such as hay or grass by the time it is a few weeks old, but in the crate this need is denied because of the undesirable iron in this natural fibrous food. (The possibility of getting iron from straw is the second reason straw is not given for bedding.) Calves, like all animals that "chew the cud," have a biological requirement for roughage; it stimulates the ruminating compartment of their digestive systems. Lack of fiber leads to diarrhea and other serious and painful digestive diseases. In the veal barn these health problems are commonplace; a direct consequence of the improper liquid diet.

Craving what the "milk replacer" lacks in nutrients, calves desperately chew on their wooden crate for small quantities of fiber and lick any metal objects they can find—nails or bucket handles—in an attempt to get the missing iron into their systems. If a calf can turn its head far enough in the crate, it will even lick its own urine for the trace amounts of iron that it contains. In addition, on the liquid diet, calves' rumens do not synthesize vitamin $B_{12}$, which makes the anemic condition even worse.

## Sick Calves

Bad food, lack of exercise, separation from the mother, denial of sucking, confinement, and the deprivation of natural social behavior—and boredom—all lead to grotesque physical and psychological debility.

These factors weaken the health of the calf and lessen its resistance to diseases such as ulcers, respiratory problems, pneumonia, septicemia, bloat, and, as already mentioned, diarrhea. But as usual, instead of improving conditions, the factory farmer resorts to regular doses of antibiotics. Calves in veal crates require five times as much medication

19. Old MacDonald's calf takes a break from gambolling in the green fields to suckle his loving mother. The sun is shining, the bell tinkles, and the mother-calf bond is strong.

as calves allowed to range free. Antibiotics kill off beneficial organisms as well as bad, so a calf fed antibiotics in its milk replacer is made not less but more vulnerable to disease. Antibiotics are also given as growth promoters, although this function of the drugs is not fully understood.

In addition to physical disease, this combination of stressful elements leads to stereotypical and neurotic behavior distress patterns, such as mouthing and tongue rolling, constant rhythmic movements, ortho-stasis—where a calf stands immobile for extended periods (an abnormal behavior pattern even though the calf may superficially appear normal and content)—hair licking in an effort to obtain roughage, and, of course, sucking—on anything within reach. In other words, the calves go crazy.

Some operators recognize that conditions in the veal crates cause the animals extreme anguish, and those who keep calves crated inside barns have a simple solution; they turn out the lights. Calves kept in darkness are calmer; and the lights are only turned on at feeding times—for the handler's convenience.

Some producers keep as many as three hundred crated calves at one time. Though not alone in the barn, each calf in its own crate is essentially in solitary confinement, with neither the comfort of its mother nor the companionship of its fellows. It is into this atmosphere and these conditions that newborn and just-days-old calves—already traumatized by the separation from their mothers and the transportation to and from the auction yards—are introduced for the duration of their short, sad, and pathetic lives.

*We generally buy our meat and poultry in neat plastic packages. It hardly bleeds. There is no reason to associate this package with a living, breathing, walking, suffering animal.*

Peter Singer, *Animal Liberation*

## Sick Meat

But the veal producer does not care about the calf's long-term health and welfare; the calf will only live about a hundred days from birth to slaughter. If 20 percent die during the ordeal, no matter, for the high price of premium "milk fed" veal takes these high losses into account—and who can tell from the meat on the plate whether the animal it came from was crazed or not?

Yet, if two out of ten calves die before slaughter from stress and disease, then clearly those which survive both the crates and the long road to the slaughterhouse must also be very sick.

## Conclusion

Like most young animals, a calf is playful, active, and naturally curious about its surroundings. It likes to run and frolic, and enjoy the social activities so important to a herd animal. But by the time it is slaughtered at sixteen weeks—barely adolescent and years before its natural life span is over—it will never have stretched its legs, run in green fields, or played with other calves. It will only escape its tiny prison when it is shipped off to be killed, the final episode of trauma, terror, and pain.

Many people feel that killing animals for food is acceptable because they believe the animals live pleasant lives in natural surroundings until they are slaughtered. Certainly, this assumption is reinforced by children's picture books of farm life and by meat industry literature

20. These three calves are chained to the front of their crates. They are lying down because it is too painful to stand on the metal rung flooring. They are nearly ready for slaughter. They have spent all of their lives in these crates.

aimed at the general public. Typically, with the best intentions, children's illustrators show the old-fashioned, more traditional situation, and typically, the industry publicity writers, who know better, aim to perpetuate this "acceptable" but out-of-date image.

If veal is a status item for the meat industry, it is also one of the most horrific examples of factory farming. "Milk fed" veal symbolizes the worst elements of this confinement system: cruelty and deprivation producing sick meat from sick animals.

# 5

# Beef Cattle

Beef cattle have never been a favorite subject for children's books—they just don't have the cuddly quality of chicks, piglets, lambs, and calves. But they often appear in secondary roles in books that glorify the "macho" spirit of the Wild West—as the raison d'être of cowboys and railroad barons.

Images of stampedes, of goring and trampling cattle, and of angry bulls pawing the ground, heads lowered and horns sharp, lend an air of danger to the handling of these large and at times almost-wild animals, and perhaps because of this, they are often seen in a slightly adversarial and threatening light.

Caring little for the fate of the cattle, we have traditionally been encouraged to root for the cowboy as he drives his herd across plains and parched deserts, and through blizzards and raging rivers. And at rodeos, indifferent to the pain and indignity inflicted on these animals, we still applaud the cowboys' bravado at the expense of those they are supposedly looking after. Even the mutilations that are regularly perpetrated upon the animals are glamorized and viewed as challenges to human prowess—cowboys must be tough and skilled to rope hundreds of unwilling calves a day, so they can be painfully branded, dehorned, and castrated.

## Beef Business

In the US, beef is a $35 billion a year industry. In 1988, the average American consumed sixty-eight pounds of beef, accounting for 7 percent of supermarket sales. This was down from the peak year of 1976, when over ninety pounds per person was the average.

Cows graze in the pasture, eating grass and clover. Some kinds of cattle are raised for the milk they give. Other kinds are beef cattle. They are raised for meat. Male cattle are called bulls or steers.

21. Old MacDonald's lucky cattle—complete with their horns—live and graze in lush pastures, "eating grass and clover." These animals, both beef and dairy, are enjoying the fresh water and shady trees. Remember this image as you look at the feedlots and dairy barns.

*The thinking man must oppose all cruel customs no matter how deeply rooted in tradition and surrounded by a halo. When we have a choice, we must avoid bringing torment and injury into the life of another, even the lowliest creature; to do so is to renounce our manhood and shoulder a guilt which nothing justifies.*

### Dr. Albert Schweitzer, *Civilization and Ethics*

To the industry's chagrin, changing tastes, better knowledge of nutrition, and medical research linking high meat consumption with many degenerative diseases have lowered the quantity of beef eaten. But, in an attempt to reverse this slide, the industry is promoting leaner beef; new ways to cut, package, sell, and serve it; and more efficient production methods—in other words, tailoring the animals' bodies and growth patterns to the latest consumer trends.

Needless to say, the 100,000 cattle slaughtered every day gain nothing from this beef merchandising campaign; they suffer from the increased pressure and abuse of being forced into factory-farming procedures where possible—or at least where profitable. While these techiques may be good for business, they are bad for animals.

Beef cattle don't "fit" into the factory-farm mold as well as other domestic animals. Unlike pigs and veal calves, no commercial advantage has been found—so far—in closely confining beef in small cages and crates. Unlike dairy cows and laying chickens, cattle yield no interim consumer products, like milk and eggs, between birth and death; producers just wait for the whole carcass. And yet, they do not escape the brutality of the factory farm.

Most beef cattle still start their lives "out on the range" in traditional manner; agribusiness happily has not yet come up with a more "efficient" way to start the production process. Unlike dairy calves, beef calves on the range often run with their mothers until they are six to eight months old. But at that age cows and calves are separated; the good breeding mothers, reimpregnated, stay on the range—and the calves and unproductive females spend the last months of their lives on feedlots.

22. A typical beef feedlot, treeless and flyblown, with feed storage elevators. Range-bred animals spend their last 100 days in this completely unnatural environment, being "finished" for slaughter.

It is true that on many smaller ranches cattle stay on the range until slaughtered. But the industry trend is more and more toward "finishing" cattle on feedlots, where producers control all factors of input and contrive the type of meat preferred by consumers.

Animals on feedlots are crowded together, denied exercise, and overfed so they gain weight fast. It used to take three years for a calf to become an adult of salable weight—now, with new finishing techniques, calves are pushed from birth through to slaughter in just ten to eleven months.

## Feedlot Life

Most outdoor feedlots are a series of small, flat, fenced fields each holding a hundred or so animals. Individual capacity varies considerably, but feedlots of over a hundred thousand head are common, with the animals crowded on the treeless, flyblown, dusty lots stretching out to the horizon.

Like chickens in battery cages, cattle on feedlots eat from a constant supply of food and water available in troughs which run along one side of the pen. There is no grass or hay given—only a high protein mix of grains, silage, and mash, with maybe some paper products, cement, chicken manure, and tallow—a beef by-product—added for bulk and good measure when the price of grain goes up. The taste of these industrial wastes—including the tallow that cynically forces cannibalism on normally vegetarian animals—must be disguised to make them palatable.

While cattle are not as crushed as in indoor lots, outdoor feedlot space is crowded and restricted. Ruminating cattle like to keep a comfortable distance from other animals; but there is no room for this natural spacing behavior. The ground in feedlots is thickly covered with excrement and often poorly drained. Cattle must stand in freezing mud and manure in winter—with no dry places to rest and chew the cud—and in summer this mixture is churned to a fine choking dust. And for cattle used to the protection from the elements given by trees and other natural features of the open range, there is usually neither shade nor shelter—and nary a clump of green grass to be seen.

Indoor feedlots or confinement buildings are more expensive for the producer to build than outdoor lots—so more demands are made on the animals to justify the high cost. The aim here is to find out how many cattle can be profitably crowded inside; the more animals enclosed, the less the per-animal cost of the facility. Yet too many animals will reduce profits—because too many will die of disease and stress. So the fine balance for the producer is the edge of suffering for the cattle.

Cattle do not thrive in a monoculture; they prefer more natural social groups of mixed ages and sexes. But feedlot operators feel there is greater efficiency and higher productivity when large numbers of items can be treated in similar fashion—like a factory assembly line. So cattle are sorted by sex, age, and anticipated slaughter date—and kept in different pens to simplify handling and eventual transportation. Their natural social behavior needs go the way of other welfare considerations.

## Sickness and Health

Grass-fed cattle have severe digestive problems when moved to feedlots—being unaccustomed to the high-protein grain and legume

23. Indoor beef raised on bare concrete slats. The industry's cynical question is, "How many animals can be crammed into the smallest space for the least cost and the greatest profit?"

diet. And hay is seldom given as an interim measure, since this involves extra labor and feed costs.

This rich food does not satisfy the cattle's biological need for roughage. The denial of this urge drives them—like crated veal calves—to lick their own and others' fur in a vain effort to get roughage. And the usual and painful results are ulcers and indigestible hairballs in the digestive system.

The sudden change from grass to grain often causes acidosis—which may bring death—since the range animals' intestinal microflora are not equipped to deal with the concentrated feedlot foods. The rich diet also causes painful abdominal bloat and laminitis, a crippling foot disease. Feedlot cattle have seven times more liver abscesses than range cattle.

In time, most cattle adjust sufficiently to feedlot food to grow and gain weight—but, of the animals dying on feedlots each year, over 10 percent succumb to digestive tract diseases. A further 60 percent,

24. An aerial view of a beef feedlot, which may hold one hundred thousand animals or more. They feed in troughs along the road into which farm trucks dump mixtures of high-protein grains and silage—and maybe recycled paper products, cement powder, and chicken manure. Because no grass or hay is given, these ruminants frequently suffer severe digestive problems.

however, die from pneumonia and other respiratory diseases caused by exposure, the high levels of dust, and lack of exercise.

Life is cheap on the feedlots; scientists report that 1 percent of cattle die before they are ready to be slaughtered. This is less than chickens, pigs, or veal calves—yet, since nearly 35 million beef cattle are slaughtered in the US every year, that 1 percent represents 350 thousand cattle who die unnecessarily and in pain due to mismanagement and poor conditions.

# Castration

Castration is carried out on cattle for the convenience of the producers, not for the good of the animals. Castration is always painful whether done surgically or nonsurgically. Castration is usually performed without anesthetics—and there is no required training and there are no laws or regulations to ensure minimum standards of procedure.

Producers castrate cattle for two reasons. First, it is believed that meat quality is improved. Second, castrated cattle, or steers, are more docile—an important factor to the owner of the crowded feedlot.

In surgical castration, the scrotum is cut open and the testes are cut off—or just pulled off. Common complications are hemorrhage, infection, tetanus, and maggot infestations.

A common method of nonsurgical castration is to place a tight rubber ring around the scrotum above the testicles—which cuts off the blood supply. After this procedure, a calf usually lies down, squirms, kicks, or swishes its tail around in pain for half an hour before the testes become numb. The atrophied part decays and weeks later, the testicles drop off.

*Non-violence leads to the highest ethics, which is the goal of all evolution. Until we stop harming all living beings, we are still savages.*

Thomas A. Edison

# Branding

Branding cattle—another glamorized cowboy occupation—identifies each animal and its owner. Unfortunately, neither branding nor ownership is permanent—and an animal may be branded over and over during its life as it is sold from ranch to auction to feedlot to slaughter.

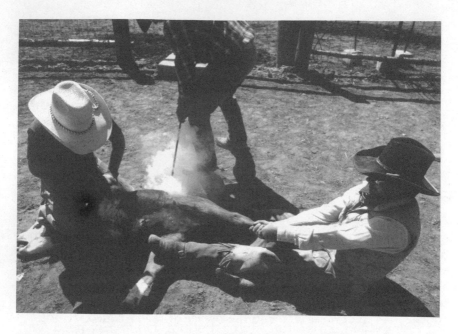

25. It takes three cowboys to turn this range-bred, almost wild calf into a defenseless, emasculated food bio-machine. Without anesthetics, calves are castrated, dehorned, ear-notched, and branded at about six months. They may be branded again and again as they are sold from ranch to auction to feedlot to slaughter.

Cruel, painful, and stressful hot branding is still used—especially out on the range. Cowboys hold heated branding irons against the hip, rib, thigh, or shoulder for three to five seconds, singeing the fur with a puff of smoke and frying the live skin. A scab forms but falls off later leaving a permanent scar. Again, no anesthetics are used.

(In 1986, in a remarkable display of cruelty and insensitivity, the US Department of Agriculture ordered over 1 1/2 million surplus dairy cows to be hot branded with a three-inch cross—on the face. Happily, public outrage caused this order to be amended, but not before many thousands had been so marked. This USDA order recalls the time several hundred years ago when adulteresses in New England were barbarously branded with a large A on the forehead.)

In freeze branding, a branding iron supercooled by liquid nitrogen is held against the animal for two minutes—freezing the skin. When the resulting dead skin falls off, the hair grows in white.

Producers are leaning towards other less-painful methods of identifying cattle, such as ear marking and even inserting electronic beepers under the skin. But as usual, it is not the intrinsic welfare of the animals that is behind this more humane trend, it is money—skins with many brand marks don't sell for as much as unmarked hides.

# Dehorning

Intensive systems of raising cattle crowd large numbers into small areas, but sharp horns can stab and injure other cattle, poke out eyes—and be dangerous to human handlers; so off they come. Horns are important weapons of defense and symbols of bovine splendor (who is not a little awed at the sight of Merrill Lynch's powerful bull?)—yet to make them fit into the factory mold, cattle must undergo this disfigurement.

Calves are dehorned with a caustic paste that chemically burns out the root of the horns. On larger animals, various knives, clippers, saws, and surgical dehorning devices are used, bloodily removing the horn, the root, and a ring of skin about one-half inch wide. Once again no anesthetics are given.

26. Tongue rolling is a "vice" in cattle. Along with rhythmic swaying, bar biting, orthostasis, and other "vices," it is a symptom of psychological distress brought on by close confinement.

For all these mutilations small calves are thrown to the ground and held down, or placed in a clamp. Larger animals are squeezed in special restraining devices. Improperly operated hydraulic "squeeze shutes" cause extensive bruising, broken necks and bones, internal injuries, and even death. Castration, branding, and dehorning are frequently all done at the same time, compounding the fear and pain—and creating an extremely traumatic experience.

The early life of beef cattle can indeed be pleasant; most grow up in open country. Yet, stress and abuse soon become constant companions—with roundup and mutilation, trucking, and auctioning, months on the feedlots, and a grim premature death at the slaughterhouse.

# Conclusion

Bulls and cows play important roles in mythology and ancient history. The fearsome man-eating Minotaur of Homer's *Odyssey* was half-man half-bull, the Egyptian goddess Hathor, motherly "queen of all gods and goddesses," had a cow's head, and in India cows have been held as sacred animals for centuries. Many nursery rhymes feature cows— jumping over the moon even—and the cow giving milk to her calf is one of the standard symbols of motherhood. Even bullfighting— however cruel it may be—glorifies the strength, bravery, and magnificient presence of the proud fighting bull.

But how the mighty have fallen! What can sad, dispirited feedlot steers still have left in common with these noble animals? We have burned our marks into their skin, cut their bodies and made them impotent, taken off their horns and left them defenseless—and crowded them together into small pens, with no regard for their grazing and roaming nature and no respect for their social and behavioral needs. We treat them as things, no more than objects to buy and sell; to be plucked out callously from among their fellows and killed and eaten whenever it suits us.

We cannot presume that animals react to stress and fear in exactly the same manner as humans. Yet if the treatment meted out to factory animals were inflicted on human beings, we could only conceive it to be possible under the most cruel, cynical, and immoral of totalitarian regimes—a thought that brings to mind similarities in the treatment of humans in concentration camps and of animals in confinement. The analogy is plain and undeniable; for both groups are held at the mercy of unfeeling keepers, deprived of freedom, crowded into small spaces,

27. This feedlot in the Midwest, deep in winter's icy slush and mud, will be churned to a fine choking dust in the heat of summer. There's no shelter from the blizzard, no shade from the sun, nowhere to lie down, and nowhere to go.

mutilated, tattooed, branded, and permanently marked, subjected to genetic experimentation—and ultimately murdered. A thought to ponder as we remember man's ongoing and irrational barbarity not only to animals but to all other life-forms on this earth.

Chickens were probably the first birds tamed by man. They provide us with eggs and meat. Some kinds are raised especially to lay eggs. Others are raised for their meat. These Brown Leghorns are raised for their eggs.

**28.** Here are some of Old MacDonald's brown leghorns feeding together in their open field. But the sight of a strutting cock is extremely rare today, since only a few males are kept in special breeding barns. All other day-old male chicks—soft and fuzzy symbols of Easter—are routinely killed by the hundreds of millions each year. They are of no use to the egg industry—they're no good for eating and they don't lay eggs.

# 6

# Chickens—
# Broilers and Layers

*A Robin Redbreast in a cage*
*Puts all Heaven in a rage.*

William Blake, *Auguries of Innocence*

*If a robin redbreast in a cage*
*Puts all heaven in a rage,*
*How feels heaven when*
*Dies the billionth battery hen?*

Spike Milligan, British comedian

Around 10,000 chickens are killed in America every minute of every day.

Over 5.4 billion chickens are slaughtered each year in the US—and in Europe, the number is 2.5 billion. The average American eats between 900 and 1,200 chickens in a lifetime; that is around 18 birds—or more than fifty-eight pounds (26 kg) of chicken—per person per year.

But sadly, only a tiny fraction—far, far less than 1 percent—of these chickens are raised on farms where they run around the barnyard, scratch in the dirt, and lead the sort of lives we recognize and remember from children's books. Those 5.4 billion chickens spend their foreshortened lives in cramped and cruel confinement. And they never see grass—let alone scratch in the dirt—from birth to death.

She loved the chick
And taught him to eat worms
And seeds and crumbs,
Peck-peck, peck-peck, peck-peck

29. "She loved the chick . . ." Old MacDonald's cozy hens taught their chicks to peck and scratch in the farmyard, and became a symbol of attentive motherhood. Sadly the reality of this image is no more, it has been replaced by . . .

Factory farms are specialist operations that usually raise just one particular species or type of farm animal; beef feedlots do not keep dairy cows; dairymen do not keep pigs; pig breeders do not keep chickens. Even chickens have been specialized; broiler hens—those raised for eating—are grown in one type of establishment, egg-laying hens in another.

Ninety to ninety-five percent of US eggs come from factory egg farms—laid by over 350 million crazed and overworked hens stuffed into small "battery cages." (In the UK the figures are 96 percent and 40–60 million.) Chickens can live up to fifteen years or more, but these caged layers are worn out after just a year and a half, crippled by the abominable conditions and forced production.

30. . . . the chick hatchery, where thousands of fertilized eggs are hatched in incubators—destined, according to breed, for the broiler house or the laying barn. These chicks will be sexed, innoculated, and shipped off around the country in plastic crates—never having seen their mother, nor heard her soft clucking.

# Hatching

"Broody" hens no longer hatch their eggs in warm and cozy straw-filled nesting boxes; fertile eggs are removed at once from the breeding hens and taken to a commercial hatchery. There they are hatched by the thousands in artificial incubators that simulate the temperature of the "broody" hen's body—but that cannot replace her well-known nurturing and mothering qualities.

Clucking and chirruping hens no longer teach their little chicks to scratch and peck for seeds, bugs, and worms, nor, as shown in the pretty pictures, do they lead them on a tour of the barnyard to meet the other animals. Little chicks never actually see their mothers; instead, at one day old, they are sorted and shipped off around the world crammed tightly into cardboard boxes and plastic crates.

Hatcheries callously expect a high death rate during the first few days, from disease, from suffocation, and from the stress of transportation, so they regularly include up to 20 percent more chicks than ordered to make up for those they know will die.

Egg farms only want female chicks; so hatcheries employ professional chicken sexers, who can handle 800–1,000 chicks an hour, to sort out and throw away the male chicks—which, unlike purpose-bred broiler chicks, are not genetically suitable for quick fattening.

Sometimes the males are gassed, crushed, or decapitated; some hatcheries have a vacuum tube system that breaks the chick's neck. A popular method—because it is cheap—is to stuff the males into large plastic bags and just let them die of suffocation. The weaker ones are trampled and die quickly; the stronger chicks fight their way to the top—and die slowly. These rejected chicks, together with the unhatched and partially hatched eggs, are ground up and the "mush" added to animal feed supplements; they may even be fed back to other chickens.

Since about as many males hatch as females, millions of day-old male chicks—little cheeping balls of yellow fluff, beloved by all children and a symbol of Easter—are uselessly destroyed every year. The slaughter of males and damaged females is intrinsic to the egg and poultry-meat industries. But these deaths are statistically irrelevant, no numbers are recorded, and almost nobody among the general public knows about their fate.

# Debeaking

From this point on, egg-laying hens and broiler hens experience very different aspects of factory farm life, except for "debeaking" which both may suffer when they arrive at their destinations.

Debeaking is the cutting off of either the entire tip of the beak or the top half of the beak, the upper mandible. A worker jams the day-old chick's beak against a red-hot (1500° F–800° C) metal blade for about two seconds. Part of the beak is burnt off and the tissue that could regenerate the beak is destroyed.

This exceptionally brutal practice cripples the chicken's primary and most sensitive tool. A chicken needs its beak for eating, pecking, preening, cleaning, and grooming, for investigating its surroundings, and for self-defense. Most debeaked chicks can still eat, though tongue burning, blistering, and overdebeaking are common; those chicks so injured often die of starvation.

The beak is not at all like a human fingernail, to which it is usually compared in poultry industry literature; the fingernail is without feeling and does not hurt when cut. The beak has a layer of highly sensitive soft tissue between the outer layer of horn and the inner bone; the red-hot debeaking knife causes severe pain, but no anesthetic is used.

Measuring pain in humans is very subjective; in animals, apart from the squawks and cries of acute pain, it is even harder. Agribusiness claims that "productivity is an infallible sign of health and general well-being." But ketosis in high-yielding dairy cows, and other production-related diseases related to fast growing pigs and broilers, belie this notion. In addition, with an instinct left over from wilder days, animals tend to hide their pain and disease lest they appear weak and easy prey for their predators.

Yet how "well an animal is doing"—whether it eats, drinks, and gains weight, and generally seems happy with its environment—may still give a rough guide to its actual state of health and happiness. We cannot tell exactly how much pain a chick feels when its beak is cut off, but it takes several days—even weeks—to recover, to resume normal growth patterns and to behave like other chicks who have not lost their beaks. At twenty weeks, some egg-layer chickens suffer the debeaking process once again, because the beak has grown back or because not enough was cut off the first time.

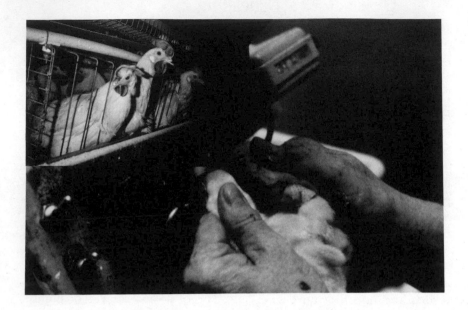

31. Every day millions of chicks are painfully "debeaked" by a red-hot knife which burns through the bone and sensitive tissue of their beaks. According to the poultry industry, debeaking prevents cannibalism, which is a natural occurrence among chickens when subjected to overcrowding and stress. Cannibalism is especially prevalent on the factory farm because of the outrageous conditions.

32. (Inset) An adult laying hen whose upper beak has been "debeaked." This disfiguring mutilation of her most useful tool lets her eat and drink, but disturbs her preening and grooming rituals.

Chickens are debeaked, as one industry educational pamphlet states, "to protect the birds from each other." Indeed, chickens in broiler factories and egg-laying cages do peck constantly at one another and may eventually kill the weaker ones. But what the pamphlet fails to say is that the overcrowding and extreme stress of the factory conditions are the real and direct causes of this abnormal and cannibalistic behavior.

*If it has eyes or runs away, don't eat it.*

Will Keith Kellogg, founder of
Kellogg breakfast cereal company

# Broiler Hens

In the broiler business, producers aim to grow the biggest bird in the shortest time for the lowest cost. That is business. But in factory-farm systems—and broiler raising is no exception—the lowest cost to the producer is usually the greatest cost to the animals, in terms of pain, suffering, and deprivation. That is cruelty.

An average broiler flock is fifty to sixty thousand birds, though many operators keep over a million birds at a single plant. Tens of thousands of broiler hens live crowded together on the floors of huge barns.

When the tiny chicks arrive, there is plenty of room; as they grow, they have progressively less room and by slaughter time each 3.5 pound (1.6 kg) bird has only half a square foot (465 sq cm) to itself—barely enough to move.

# The Pecking Order

A factor of major importance in a chicken's life is the security of her place in the "pecking order"; this social structure formalizes relationships between individuals. In Old MacDonald's barnyard, the senior cock and senior hen establish a ranking order that allows each hen to lead a happy and ordered life—except for the lowest hen on the totem pole, although in the open barnyard even she has room to get out of everybody's way.

But in the broiler barn in the social chaos of thousands of milling chickens, the immediate group is constantly changing. There are too many birds for this instinctively needed and well-defined order to develop. And without the security of the pecking order, normal behavior patterns are impossible and individuals become stressed, disoriented, hysterical, and aggressive to their neighbors.

# Day and Night, Night and Day

Broiler-house lighting is constantly manipulated. Producers may make cycles of darkness and light as short as one hour of "day" and three hours of "night"; more frequent "nights" and "days" stimulate higher food consumption and, theoretically, faster weight gain. In other methods of inducing constant feeding and speeding weight gain, the lights may be kept on for twenty-three hours straight.

But this manipulation of light strains the biological time clock that regulates a chicken's daily rhythms. Different animals sleep in varying amounts and at different times of the day and night, but all life regulates its functions by the sun. Upsetting these circadian cycles causes distress, and the ill effects on humans of disturbing the natural daily rhythms—jet lag is just one example—are well established; in fact, the manipulation of time is used as an instrument of torture. Yet this treatment is meted out continuously to broiler hens—to turn the chickens' misery to monetary advantage.

33. The stench of ammonia, the dust, and the overcrowding in a broiler hen house are extreme. As the fifty-six days of its short life pass in the darkened barn, the growing broiler chick has almost no room to move and no place to perch.

# Disease

Huge numbers of stressed chickens massed together are very susceptible to disease. They can be wiped out in a few days by the rapid
spread of diseases like avian flu, but most often they suffer from serious
health problems associated with factory-farm conditions; for example,
respiratory diseases due to the high levels of dust and ammonia in the
air; "litter burned" skin from the high moisture and ammonia content
of the waste on the floor; Marek's disease, a cancer linked to the stress
of overcrowding and accelerated growth. Marek's disease, in fact, is
the major reason some 140,000 tons of poultry meat is condemned
annually by slaughterhouse inspectors—that is equivalent to 80–100
million chickens' lives wasted a year.

Many birds simply cannot stand the strain, and die of "sudden death
syndrome" or "flip-over," as the industry calls it; the chickens let out a
last squawk, then flip onto their backs and die.

As usual on factory farms, the solution is to medicate everybody, just
in case. And as with other factory animals, the indiscriminate dosing of
broiler hens with large amounts of drugs results in residues in the meat.

*Yet saddest of all fates surely, is to have lost that
sense of the holiness of life altogether, that we
commit the blasphemy of bringing thousands of
lives to a cruel and terrifying death, or of making
those lives a living death—and feel nothing.*

The Right Reverend John Austin Baker,
Bishop of Salisbury

# Off to Market

When they reach about 3.5 pounds (1.6 kg), these young chickens are
"ready"; they are grabbed roughly by their feet, carried upside down
two or three chickens in each of the worker's hands, stuffed into plastic
crates and loaded onto trucks. One semitrailer alone can haul six
thousand chickens on the traumatic trip to the slaughterhouse.

"We use everything but the cackle!" goes the macabre industry
boast; but there is seldom a cackle to be heard from the catatonic birds
who huddle in the crates stacked at the slaughterhouse and await their
turn to be slaughtered.

Indeed no part is wasted; after the carcasses are dressed and neatly and innocuously packaged, the remains—the head, feet, entrails, blood, and feathers—are dried, ground up, and sold as "poultry by-products" for pet food and other animal feeds. Even diseased and cancerous chickens are not thrown away; their carcasses are chopped up, the bad bits cut out and the "good" parts collected and sold as "chicken pieces" and "chicken wings."

The life of broiler chickens is marked by mutilation, overcrowding, and stress, but the welfare of the birds for their own sake is not a consideration for the producer; he apparently only cares about suffering and pain among the chickens if they affect the efficiency of his operation.

At least a broiler's agony is short; the bird, whose natural life span is over fifteen years, is killed before it is barely sixty days old. But the broiler's egg-laying cousins must endure worse conditions—for at least a year, sometimes two—before they are worn out and sent to slaughter.

# Egg Layers

Egg industry publications state proudly that most of America's eggs come fresh from farms in the country; but for the caged factory layers who produce 95 percent of all US eggs, country life is a life sentence in a closed barn. These chickens never in their entire lives run outside, scratch for a worm, take a dust bath, feel a country breeze ruffle their feathers, savor the sun on their backs—or even hear the early morning crowing of a cock. Being "in the country" defines the producer's life-style—not theirs.

In Britain, the Protection of Birds Act (1954) prohibits a parrot or other pet bird from being kept in a cage so small it cannot spread its wings. Yet this same law turns a blind eye to laying hens—as does the Animal Welfare Act in the United States.

The average wingspan of a chicken is thirty-two inches (80 cm); the average size of a battery cage is eighteen inches by twelves inches (45 cm × 30 cm). But egg-factory operators are permitted to cram not just one, but up to five full-grown chickens into a cage too small to allow even one bird alone to stretch her wings. And there the hens stay for a year or more.

Cage sizes vary from country to country and manufacturer to manufacturer. Some are designed for up to nine birds, some for only three. There is no standard cage, only an average cage. All include tight confinement as an integral part.

34. This is just one aisle in a laying house that holds sixty thousand birds or more—squeezed together in three or four tiers of battery cages. The clamoring cackles and churning movement are ceaseless. After a year or two, these "spent layers" will be slaughtered for soup and pet food.

35. The wingspan of a chicken is about 30–32". The average battery cage measures 18" × 15"; flapping or stretching is impossible for one hen, let alone when there are four or five cage mates. Flying is also out of the question. Although they spend most of their time on the ground searching for food, chickens in open surroundings often fly up on to tree branches or barn beams to perch at night.

While such anomalies in the law may not surprise us, they cannot justify the conditions of extreme physical and psychological abuse in which egg-laying chickens are "housed."

The egg industry claims that the laying hen copes well with the stress of the cage since she continues to lay eggs—about 250 a year. Yet laying eggs, especially when stimulated by drugs, food additives, and other manipulations of her existence, becomes a metabolic necessity for a hen; she will accomplish this despite the worst obstacles.

# Inside the Cage

Battery cages are stacked in long rows three to five tiers or more high (one European company builds egg battery barns with cages stacked two *stories* high). Water and food are available in troughs running in front of the cages.

Cages are made of wire mesh on the top, bottom, and all four sides, with a one-in-five gradient floor. The sloping floor lets the eggs roll to the front for easy collection—easy for the farmer—but it makes it impossible for the birds to perch or lay eggs comfortably.

Chicken's feet become crippled and malformed from living on the wire mesh. They are often found with their toenails inextricably entwined in the floor; sometimes the flesh of their toes grows completely around the wire. If they get trapped away from the food and water, they die—of thirst and starvation.

With only four chickens in a 12″ × 18″ (30 cm × 45 cm) cage, each bird has about fifty-four square inches—or an area 6″ × 9″ (350 sq cm) to itself. Most laying hens are larger than that, so there is never a time when an individual is not being crushed up against—or under—her cell mates. When one moves, they must all move.

The cage churns constantly as birds seeking more space trample on their cell mates; backs become raw from claws and from being pecked—for even debeaked hens do damage over time.

In a battery cage low-ranking birds cannot get away from or show submission to their seniors; so a state of confrontation, fear, and frustration rules. Weaker birds may never get off the bottom of the cage; they will die of suffocation, unable to struggle to the top—or, like some of their broiler-hen sisters, they will just give up and die without any apparent cause.

Over the months, feathers become ragged and blisters develop from the continual rubbing against the wire and the unending competition to get up where there is more space and cooler air. By the time the birds are "retired" to the slaughterhouse, most have almost no feathers left.

*If we learn to be compassionate towards other forms of life, we may learn to become compassionate to our own species. We may become humane —at long last.*

Farley Mowat, author of "Never Cry Wolf" and long-time naturalist writer and campaigner in defense of wildlife

## Laying Rituals Disrupted

Dutch scientists report that hens in traditional henhouses in the privacy of straw-lined nesting boxes take an average of 16.4 minutes from the beginning of their nesting and prelaying behavior to the actual laying of the egg; battery-cage hens, with *only one* other cage mate, take an average of 74.2 minutes.

The frightened battery hen starts to panic as she vainly searches for privacy and a suitable nesting place in the crowded but bare wire cage; then she appears to become oblivious to her surroundings, struggling against the cage as though trying to escape. Eventually she manages to lay her egg. Indeed, the constant squawking cacophony of frenzied hens in the egg factory contrasts harshly with the relatively quiet clucking of the old-fashioned henhouse.

Take a moment to imagine yourself as a layer chicken; your home is a crowded cage with a wire floor that causes your feet to hurt and become deformed; there's no room to stretch your legs or flap your wings and they become weak from lack of exercise; but at the same time, you can never be still because there is always one of your miserable cell mates who needs to move about; one of the other chickens is always picking on you and you cannot get away—except by letting others sit on top of you; the air is filled with dust and flying feathers that stick to the sides of the cage splattered with chicken shit from the inmates in the cages upstairs; it is hard to breathe—there is a choking stench of ammonia in the air from the piles of manure under the cages and you don't feel at all well; the flies are unbearable despite the insecticide sprayed in the air and laced in your food—to kill the fly larvae before they mature; the food—never green and fresh—seldom varies and tastes always of the chemical additives and drugs needed to keep you alive; eventually, despite your wretchedness and anguish, and the tormented din of thousands of birds shrieking their pain together, you lay an egg and watch it roll out of sight; but the joy of making a nest, of giving birth, of clucking to your chicks is absent—laying the

Every day the little red hen laid a beautiful white egg.

36. Old MacDonald's little red hen probably took about 15–20 minutes to go through her laying rituals in the peace and quiet of her straw-lined nest. According to researchers, her factory-farm counterpart takes about 70 agonizing minutes of psychological and physical frustration and interruption in her crowded cage to produce her so-called "country-farm-fresh egg."

egg is an empty, frustrating, and exhausting ritual. Rumor has it there are another three hundred days of this—might as well give up and die now while you still have some feathers.

Even as you read this, 350 million egg-laying hens are suffering in battery cages in the US—and many millions more chickens around the world are existing in similar conditions.

## Death and Disease

Up to 20 percent of the laying flock commonly die before they are sold as "spent hens" to the soup and pet food factories—at forty-three cents a head. While some of the old diseases are largely conquered, new ones—"diseases of intensification"—have proliferated. Chick-

37. In a cage like this, with wire floors which deform their feet, four or five laying hens are crammed together for a year or more—or until they wear out and die. An American Egg Board educational publication would have us believe these cages were "actually designed for the welfare of the birds."

38. (Inset) The feathers of this laying hen, like the three on the front cover, have been plucked out or worn down to the shaft by months of constant rubbing against the wire cages.

ens die from infectious bronchitis, from egg peritonitis, from cannibalism, from sheer exhaustion, from diseases resulting from immunological weakness caused by overspecialized breeding, and often from CLF—caged layer fatigue—in which they use up the minerals in their bones and muscles until they can no longer stand.

Feeding, watering, egg-and-manure removal systems can be completely automatic; it takes one worker just a few hours every day to manage 70,000 to 100,000 hens and give them their regular doses of medication. But there is no time in the day for the sick and injured to get individual attention; only time for the dozens of dead and dying to be collected. In some factories these dead birds are hydrolyzed, ground up, sterilized, and fed right back to the others.

It is typical of the industry's moral numbness that producers encourage, indeed force, cannibalism on the hens, while at the same time, they cut off their beaks to prevent it. It is all a matter of dollars and cents, because the hen, that paragon of nurturing motherhood on Old MacDonald's Farm, is now just an egg-laying machine; to be oiled with antibiotics when it shows signs of breaking down, and to be cannibalized for spare parts or sold for scrap—chicken soup—when it finally wears out.

Yet this "machine," this specialized animal bred expressly for caged productivity, despite all her anguish and pain, despite all that man has done to her, still retains the instincts of the old-fashioned hen. Research in England with freed battery chickens shows that hens, even after two years of incarceration—unless they are too sick or too weak to stand—will immediately scratch in the dirt for worms and bugs, choose a secluded place to lay their eggs, perch, take dust baths, sunbathe, and form a community life.

Can it be any clearer? The broiler house and the battery cage are truly gross forms of abuse, deprivation, and cruelty to hens.

# 7

# Transportation

Children's books about farm life show animals being born, growing up, and living on the farm, but rarely do they clearly explain where the animals go after the farm. Because of this, the subject of transporting animals from place to place is also seldom mentioned—except, briefly, when some animals leave the farm and go "off to market."

Picture-book animals "go off to market" by various means; sometimes they are rounded up and herded off by cowboys, sometimes they are led quietly away on a string; in old-fashioned books they are taken in carts; but more often these days, animals are shown loaded onto pickup trucks.

But their destination is only lightly alluded to, and the full import of the final fate of farm animals is glossed over; it is almost as though once the animals have left the storybook farm, there is little more to say about them. The child is left with the impression that "off to market" means either the animals, implausibly, are going shopping to buy groceries or, more believably, that they will be sold to another farmer, to spend the rest of their lives at a different farm. The truth, of course, is that the animals are going to auction yards or slaughterhouses.

Very few factory-farm animals are born and die on the same farm. This means that practically all animals are transported at least once, while most animals—especially cattle—are trucked several times in their lives—from farm to feedlot, from auction yard to holding yard, from hatchery to henhouse. In the end, they all travel on a one-way ticket to the slaughterhouse.

Ninety-five percent of all animals today are transported in trucks and semitrailers, which are designed to move the maximum number of animals as quickly and as cheaply as possible. Only a small percentage go by ship or rail—though when billions of animals are involved, a small percentage represents many millions. Whether taken by truck, rail, or ship, travel is no joyride.

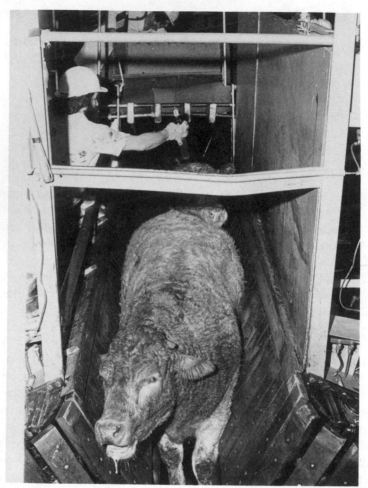

39. Well over one hundred thousand head of cattle meet this fate at the slaughterhouse each day in the US. Some packing houses have "kill rates" of 400 animals an hour. "The worst sin towards our fellow creatures is not to hate them, but to be indifferent to them. That's the essence of inhumanity."—*George Bernard Shaw*

*I am in favor of animal rights as well as human rights. That is the way of a whole human being.*

Abraham Lincoln

# The Law

Sadly, the Animal Welfare Act, the only major federal legislation that generally regulates the treatment of animals in the US, specifically excludes from its mandate, among other omissions, the transportation of animals used for food or fiber. The government can regulate the way you travel with your dog on a plane, but not the way you send your pig, cow, or chicken to market.

There are thousands of dogs, cats, household pets, wild animals, birds, and zoo animals who need care and attention during transportation and who come under the protection of the act. But the billions of farm animals—who can suffer just as much as the others from miserable transport conditions—stand outside the protective law.

There is a federal requirement that animals in transit be fed, watered, and rested at least every twenty-eight hours. But, unfortunately, this twenty-eight-hour law only applies to those animals transported by rail or ship.

Congress has repeatedly failed to pass amendments to include within this twenty-eight-hour law the vast majority of animals moved by truck. (The Humane Society of the US has verified that some truck trips across the country last up to sixty hours.) So millions of animals are trucked every day with little control over their welfare—except what is in the financial self-interest of the owners and operators.

Some state laws regulate local transportation conditions, but the main arbiter of transportation criteria for animal welfare is the industry itself—and there the essential motivation is economics, not compassion. The death of animals in transit from disease, injury, and abuse is tolerated because this loss is built into the profit structure and can be absorbed without economic hardship. And so the plight of the hundreds of thousands of injured, abused, and dead victims who end up as transportation casualties is a minor factor in the industry's calculations.

# Disease and Injury

Government studies show that more than 700,000 calves and cattle die each year due to transit-related injuries and diseases. Each day nearly 2,000 dead or injured cattle, calves, sheep, goats, pigs, and horses are rejected at federally inspected slaughterhouses.

One-and-a-half million chickens and turkeys are condemned annually at processing plants due to injuries that make them unfit for human consumption. Such figures reveal that the present state of livestock

40. These pigs await slaughter in California. They will have traveled hours in crowded, poorly ventilated trucks without food or water—or perhaps days in a train from the Midwest. The Animal Welfare Act has afforded them little protection on their long journey.

transportation is unquestionably cruel and incredibly wasteful of life. And for every animal that shows up in the statistics, there are many more with lesser injuries who have suffered the same abusive, terrifying experiences.

While the family dog loves going in the car with his head out the window, the family cat usually meows pitifully the whole trip, scratching to get out or lying in torpid fear on the floor. Like the cat, most animals are frightened by the novelty of being on an unstable moving surface. They don't understand what is happening, their senses are confused, and, unlike the dog, they don't have the affectionate attention of their human companions.

But fear of the unfamiliar motion of the truck is only one cause of distress. There are more serious problems that affect all animals in transit and others that specifically affect different species.

On extended trips animals are frequently neither fed nor watered;

there are no fast-food places for animals in transit. Trucking companies do not want to spend the time, money, or effort to offload the animals, care for them and load them up again—even if there were convenient places for them to do this—and the trucks are too crowded to provide feed and water on board.

Animals who have lived all their lives in climate-controlled factory-farm buildings may suddenly have to spend prolonged periods in the heat or the cold. There can be extreme changes in humidity and temperature over long distances too. Animals from a cool climate suffer when moved to hot and humid regions—and vice versa.

Truck design aims to maximize capacity, rather than to provide comfortable accommodation. But animals are not packed in tightly just to reduce the transport cost per animal; loosely loaded animals fall about on curves and sudden stops, and can get hurt. On crowded trucks, ventilation is often poor and animals in the middle sometimes suffocate.

Additional hazards are bad roads, inclement weather, heavy traffic, and mechanical breakdowns.

Injuries result from fighting when animals from one group are mixed and crushed together with unfamiliar animals from different groups or farms. Without time to adjust to each other's company, fear leads to aggressive behavior.

Cuts and bruises heal up in time—although they affect meat quality at the slaughterhouse if the animals are headed that way. But some animals receive serious physical injuries—such as broken legs and broken pelvises—and fall down in the truck. Other animals slip on the slick surface of the truck bed and cannot get up because of lameness, weak legs, or just plain exhaustion. Once down, these "spreaders" and "downers" are further injured—even trampled to death—by the other animals.

## Loading/Unloading and Auction Yards

Loading and unloading from trucks—or ships and trains—is a terrifying series of events since it is completely foreign to the animal's normal experience. Range cattle, used to open spaces, are suddenly crammed together first in the stockyards, then in the trucks. Factory-farm animals with heavy bodies and weak legs, who have been confined all their lives—and prohibited from exercising in order to promote weight gain—are suddenly forced to run up and down steep and slippery ramps, jump in and out of trucks, and negotiate chutes, fences, and

41. In the background, thousands of crated broiler hens wait their turn. They will be grabbed by their feet, strung upside down on the processing line, and funneled towards the knife that slits their throats.

gates at high speed. Unloading is usually worse than loading because the animals are tired and weakened by the journey.

Almost all auction yards are overcrowded and animals are moved through quickly at any cost. Here, the trauma of loading, trucking, and unloading is compounded by brutal, insensitive, and sometimes inexperienced handlers who shout, kick, beat, and poke. Young, old, lame, and sick animals endure the harshest treatment; stockyard workers batter them with heavy canes and jab electric prods in their ears and genital areas to get them to move faster.

Downers, spreaders, calves barely able to walk, and other injured animals who cannot move are dragged off the trucks with ropes and chains. One end of the rope is tied around the head or a leg—even a broken one—the other end to a post in the ground. Then the truck is driven away and the animal skids along the truck bed until it crashes to the ground. Dairy cows who become downers or spreaders while "on the job" are moved from the farm to the slaughterhouse by similar methods.

Injured animals are dragged away and piled up in a heap in an out-of-the-way place. They may wait without veterinary care—or water—for hours or days before being put out of their misery. First, a Federal Meat and Poultry Inspector must decide whether or not they are fit for humans to eat, and if they are, then they must be killed by a designated butcher. If condemned, they will join the animals dead on arrival and become pet food.

Animals arriving dead at the slaughterhouse are also rejected for human consumption, but others are accepted however sick they may be as long as they can walk through the door. When they are dead, boned out, and ground up, who can tell the difference?

Female animals are often found to be pregnant when killed; in fact, some operators deliberately impregnate their slaughterhouse-bound cows and sows to increase their weight at sale time. However well-developed they may be, the fetuses do not survive—but there is a cozy trade in piglet fetuses; about half are big enough for classroom dissections, retailing at about four to five dollars each.

As mentioned before, the industry recoups the economic loss of animals injured and dead in transit by adjusting the final price of the meat. While the best price for the meat is obtained in the supermarket, the incentive to maximize income by improving conditions and reducing transport losses is nonexistent because even condemned and "dead-on-arrival" animals fetch an adequate price. They may not be "fit" for human consumption but they are fine for the pet food industry, and other by-products—hides, bones, collagen, etc.—are also valuable. Even the wastes, the blood, entrails, and cancerous remains of slaughtered animals are rendered in a dry melter into a dry powder that is fed back to factory animals as a protein supplement.

With the existence of this related market, the transportation side of the meat industry has little financial motivation to improve the lot of the animals. And clearly, the meat industry will fight hard against any legislation on behalf of the animals that will change the old ways, recognize that animals have some legitimate rights, and, most of all, incur large expenditures merely to increase animal welfare.

*To us it seems incredible that the Greek philosophers should have scanned so deeply into right and wrong and yet never noticed the immorality of slavery. Perhaps 3,000 years from now it will seem equally incredible that we do not notice the immorality of our own oppression of animals.*

Brigid Brophy, British novelist

## Chickens in Transit

Up to 10 percent of chickens die in transport.

Chickens who spend their entire lives in controlled environments at even temperatures are crammed into small cages and crates, then stacked onto open trucks, exposed to all variations of weather from winter blizzards to summer heat waves. In hot weather, crowded birds in the inside cages suffocate.

Many chickens are injured or bruised while being caught by their feet and loaded for removal to the slaughterhouse. One company invented a large vacuum machine to speed the loading of chickens. The chickens are sucked out of their cages and pass through long tubes to the waiting trucks. Apart from the chickens' extreme panic caused by this grotesque method of handling, users report as many injuries as with hand catching.

*My life is full of meaning to me. The life around me must be full of significance to itself. If I am to expect others to respect my life, then I must respect the other life I see. Ethics in our Western world has hitherto been largely limited to the relations of man to man. But that is a limited ethics. We need a boundless ethics which will include the animals also.*

Dr. Albert Schweitzer, *Civilization and Ethics*

## Pigs in Transit

Pigs raised in confinement are more susceptible to the ordeal of transportation stress than field-reared pigs. But all are traumatized by being mixed in with unfamiliar groups; stress-related acute dilation of the heart is a major cause of pigs' death while in transit.

In the UK, the Meat and Livestock Commission reported that of 10,000 pigs examined after transit, over 50 percent were "damaged" and 44 percent were injured in fighting. Injuries were caused by bad lighting, poor segregation, overcrowding, excessively steep ramps, and overuse of electric prods.

# Cattle and Calves

Beef cattle tend to be shipped more often than other animals; producers may not be satisfied with the price offered at auction and take them elsewhere. Thus animals may often make several trips to auctions before ending up on a feedlot or farm.

Furthermore, some brokers and speculators buy animals cheap at one auction and then turn around and sell them at another. These animals are under constant stress from the transportation and the frequent changing of location. As a result, producers see reduced "performance" in recently shipped animals.

The trauma of shipping is made worse for cattle and calves fresh off the range by the practice of weaning, dehorning, and castration just

42. To be considered fit for human consumption an animal must be able to walk through the packing house door. Some of those that make it are kept going till slaughter on large doses of antibiotics. Here are three out of thousands every day who arrive dead. The loss of those animals too sick or too injured to survive transportation is built into the industry's profit structure.

prior to transit, sometimes on the same day. This combination of stressors often causes "shipping fever pneumonia," the major reason cattle die in transit.

The newly born calf is one of the animals least able to stand the stress of shipment. Yet dairy calves are hauled to auction yards and then to their new "homes" within a week of birth.

PSE meat (*p*ale, *s*oft, and *e*xudative) in pigs and "dark cutter" meat from cattle are poor-quality meats that are directly the result of stress in shipping and handling. Pneumonia, gastric ulcers, and gastroenteritis are other common transport-related diseases.

## International Shipping of Live Animals

Overseas trade in live food animals is a lucrative business for countries with excess livestock, but involves conditions of extreme crowding and deprivation over extended periods of time. For example, unwanted dairy calves—only days old—are shipped across the often-rough seas of the English Channel by ferry and truck to factory veal farms in European countries where veal is more in demand, on journeys that may take several days.

But perhaps most horrific is the sheep trade from Australia and New Zealand to the Middle East, where animal-welfare legislation is almost unheard of and where treatment of animals by ship's crew, dock workers, and slaughterhouse men is known to be particularly inhumane and cruel.

Seven million sheep a year are crammed—3 per square yard—on ships specially outfitted to carry up to 100,000 animals at one time. Other major stress factors—and causes of vast numbers of deaths— are poor ventilation across equatorial waters where temperatures are high, lack of sufficient clean feed and water, and gastric infections. Dead sheep—as well as the sick and injured—are thrown overboard to waiting sharks.

These sea journeys last from three to five weeks and cover up to eight thousand miles. On one voyage in 1985 between Australia and Saudi Arabia, extreme heat and humidity killed 15,000 sheep out of a total of 90,000; on more "normal" voyages a 5 percent loss is common.

Those sheep dying at sea may be the lucky ones—the rest face a brutal off-loading process and then trucking to *hal-al* slaughterhouses where Moslem ritual slaughter forbids stunning before killing. Sheep are thrown on their backs on the floor, or on special racks, and held down while their throats are cut. Or they may be shackled by their rear legs and hoisted—alive but upside down—to await the butcher's knife.

*There is no religion without love, and people may talk as much as they like about their religion, but if it does not teach them to be good and kind to beasts as well as man, it is all a sham.*

Anna Sewell, *Black Beauty*

## Conclusion

An industry that produces so many animals a year for food must use mass-transport systems to move them around. Such systems must inevitably be stressful to the animals and result in disease and injury. It is hard to see how the demands of the system and the minimum needs of the animals can be reconciled, but certainly no improvement will be made until Congress and governments in other countries enact appropriate legislation. More importantly, until the meat industry acknowledges the welfare of animals as an end in itself, there will continue to be little compassion in the treatment of animals. The fact is, animals are given more care and consideration when they are dead—as carcass meat—than when they are alive.

43.  One man's meat . . . . During a lifetime, the average American will eat all the
animals pictured on this page.

# 8

# Medical Import for Humans

Of the two million people who will die in the US this year, an incredible 70 percent will have suffered and died from the three chronic killer diseases: cancer, stroke, and heart attacks—each day 764 people die from heart attacks.

In the UK, over 50 percent of deaths are due to heart attacks, stroke, hypertension, and other circulatory diseases. The critical fact is that these and other degenerative diseases—from which still more millions are crippled each year—have been linked conclusively to consumption of beef and other animal products.

Meat has always been part of man's diet since the earliest of times, goes the oft-heard argument. So why should he not continue to eat it, since from long-standing habit and tradition at least, meat is his natural food? Leaving aside the ethics of killing animals to eat, there are some telling reasons.

First, modern meats may be up to seven times as fat as prehistoric meat, and contain five times less polyunsaturated fat. Modern meats are even different from the meats of only one hundred years ago when genetic engineering and scientifically selective breeding for specialized, meatier body types were unknown, and the animals were not subjected to the misery and stress of confinement, overcrowding, and denial of natural behavior in factory farms.

Second, modern meat may be laced with residues from all the drugs and chemical additives the animals have ingested during the course of their lives—and the full consequences for humans of this long-term low dosage through their food is not yet known.

And thirdly—and most importantly—in the industrialized "rich" world more meat is being eaten than ever before. According to the 1989 USDA statistics, total animal-derived food consumption in the

US, for instance, is now over 800 pounds per year for each man, woman, and child, including 68 pounds of beef, 244 eggs, 44 pounds of pork, 57 pounds of poultry and dairy products equivalent to some 70 gallons of milk.

The many studies that compare the so-called normal diets of Western societies with the diets of different countries, races, and other clearly defined, statistically useful groups point to the conclusion that there is a direct relationship between the consumption of meat and the incidence of degenerative diseases such as the three mentioned above and many others such as diabetes, bowel cancer, multiple sclerosis, obesity, and kidney disease. These diseases of excess are rampant in the rich, developed world, with certain exceptions, but almost unknown in the planet's poorer areas where slow death through nutritional deficiency and starvation are more common. Here are a few examples.

The Seven Countries study, an international study involving some twelve and a half thousand men in Japan, the US, and five countries in Europe, revealed a clear correlation between heart disease and the intake of saturated fats—meat was the main source of saturated fats in their diet. A study in Israel conducted between 1949 and 1977 confirmed that death from coronary disease increased as Israelis ate more and more meat. In California, a study at Loma Linda University of eighteen thousand people who ate no meat showed an incidence of heart attacks only 15 percent of the national rate.

Members of the Seventh-Day Adventist Church provide a handy statistical group for comparison with the "norm," since as a group they are essentially similar in all respects to the general population of the US except in their diet. Most, because of religious philosophy, eat very little meat and about 50 percent eat no meat at all. A study of some 27,500 Seventh-Day Adventists showed a close relationship between meat consumption and death from heart disease, pointing out that the more meat and poultry is eaten, the greater the risk of death from heart disease. Note that poultry is included as contributing to "mortality risk" even though it is generally considered low in saturated fat.

These and other studies all tell the same story: the more meat, the more heart disease–related death. The American Heart Association is now recommending a diet low in animal fat as a precaution against heart disease. While all the subtle connections between meat consumption and heart disease are not yet completely understood, one ingredient of animal-derived food which is known to play a major role is cholesterol.

The human body makes and needs cholesterol in small amounts for the production of certain bodily fluids, but excessive cholesterol accumulation on the artery walls is a prime suspect in heart disease. Some foods, like the caffeine in coffee, stimulate the body to produce it, but of the all the foods we eat, *only animal-derived foods* actually contain cholesterol. By age 4, the average US child already has a level of serum cholesterol that is as high as an adult's should get if the adult is to avoid coronary plaque buildup, and about 30 percent of children have levels of cholesterol which most experts agree are abnormally high.

A Finnish study, which modified the diet of a test group for a certain period, showed that lower cholesterol in the blood could be induced by cutting back on meat and saturated fat in the diet—and just as significantly, that a return to the former diet brought serum cholesterol back up to previous levels.

Incidentally, actively lowering cholesterol is as important as not raising it; for every 1 percent drop in cholesterol levels, there is a possible 2 percent drop in heart disease risk.

Hypertension—or excessively elevated blood pressure—has also been shown to correlate closely with meat consumption. This disease is known as the silent killer because of the lack of symptoms.

# Diabetes

Diabetes is another degenerative disease that is related to high fat content in the diet—not just to the excessive consumption of sugars, which is the popular belief. Statistically, every fifth American will have diabetes at some point in his life.

A University of Minnesota study of some 25,700 members of the Seventh-Day Adventist Church showed a close correlation between meat consumption and diabetes. Those eating meat more than six times a week had nearly four times the likelihood of contracting diabetes than those who never ate meat.

*We don't eat anything that has to be killed for us. We've been through a lot and we've reached a stage where we really value life.*

Paul McCartney

# Cancers

Rates of cancer are rising. In 1981, the National Cancer Institute estimated one third of the US population would develop cancer at some point in their lives. Other researchers believe that if present rates continue, 50 percent will have cancer by the year 2000 and few will escape the disease in the twenty-first century. A grim forecast.

Numerous epidemiological studies have linked increasing consumption of beef, meat, and saturated fat with rising rates of cancer. One comprehensive report suggests that 35 percent of all cancer deaths are diet related. A few samples.

In one seven-year survey, scientists found that among some 35,000 members of the Seventh-Day Adventist Church in the US, the death rate from all cancers was only 53 percent of the national average. This was attributed partly to their low meat diet. The Israeli study on heart disease mentioned above indicated also that deaths from all malignant cancers increased during the years 1949 to 1977, coinciding with the rising rate of animal fat intake.

Multinational studies comparing average meat and saturated fat content of national diets have shown that the more meat in the diet, the higher the number of deaths from intestinal cancer per head of population, with Japan at the bottom of the list and heavy meat-eating Canada, the US, and New Zealand at the top. In case anybody might think there was a racial bias against this type of cancer in ethnic Japanese, another study compared incidence of colon cancer in Japanese living in Japan with ethnic Japanese resident in the US. It was shown that those Japanese in the US eating the meatier US-style diet were three times as likely to contract colon cancer as the Japanese in Japan with their traditional low meat diet. It should be noted, however, that breast and colon cancer are increasing in Japan as the traditional diet gives way to the high fat meat and dairy diet of the West.

Other studies of women have related ovarian cancer to fat consumption, and breast cancer to eating beef and pork. In Thailand, breast cancer in women and prostate cancer in men are rare, while they are increasing in those countries in North America and Europe in which people have a high animal fat diet.

While epidemiological connections between meat eating and all forms of cancer are clear, the exact mechanism that may induce cancer in the heavy meat consumer is not perfectly understood. Among the possible factors, one likely contributing candidate is the lack of fiber in meat. Without fiber, the intestinal tract may not be able to rid the body efficiently of toxins, thus permitting the accumulation of carcinogenic substances. And there is encouraging evidence that eating starchy vegetables, beans, and vegetables with plenty of fiber, only found in plant foods, may offer protection against cancers.

Some cancers may be transmitted by virus from one species to another, i.e., from animals to humans, and some animals slaughtered for food certainly have cancer—chickens with Marek's disease, for instance. But not all cancerous animals are rejected at the slaughterhouse, as we shall see, and even when cancers are found, the rest of the carcass, with tumors removed, is shipped to supermarkets, wholesalers, and fast-food outlets. A government report states that over 90 percent of chickens from most of the flocks in this country and abroad are infected with leukosis (chicken cancer) even though only a smaller percentage develop overt neoplasms or tumors.

One ten-ounce charcoal-grilled steak contains as much of the powerful carcinogen benzopyrene as 170 cigarettes. Pork and cured meats often contain nitrites that combine with other substances in the human body to form nitrosamines, a most potent nervous system carcinogen. Disturbing evidence now links some brain tumors in children with high prenatal nitrite consumption by their mothers.

These are just some of the connections between high meat consumption and cancer. As meat consumption has increased in industrialized countries since World War II, so have rates of cancer. And as rates of meat consumption have gone up, so have the numbers of animals raised in factory farms. And so too have the quantities of drugs, pesticides, and other chemicals that have been added to the feeds and medication given to animals on modern meat-raising facilities. We will take a look at the possible harmful effects on humans of this aspect of intensive confinement.

*Grant animals a ray of reason, imagine what a frightful nightmare the world is to them: a dream of cold-blooded men, blind and deaf, cutting their throats, slitting them open, gutting them, cutting them into pieces, cooking them alive, sometimes laughing at them and their contortions as they writhe in agony. Is there anything more atrocious among the cannibals of Africa?*

Romain Rolland, Nobel Prize winner,
"Jean Christophe"

## Drug Residues in Meat

Disease-inducing saturated fats and cholesterol are found in meats wherever they come from, but other harmful and toxic ingredients found in most meat today are the result of factory-farming methods. The meat eater, at the top of the food chain, receives the full impact. He consumes a varied accumulation of chemical residues from the large quantities of antibiotics, growth stimulants, mold inhibitors, pesticides, and other additives that the meat animal has eaten during the course of its life. This ingested chemical potpourri renders once-helpful drugs ineffective, contributes to cancerous disorders, and generally weakens human defenses against disease. The kidneys of a modern meat eater, for instance, must continually work overtime to deal with the toxic wastes found in his meat.

Worse, our children, with the blessings of government, agriculture, and big business, are being insidiously harmed by this chemical pollution on a daily basis; an increasing number of children's lives are being disrupted by chemically induced allergies and intolerances. Incidence of asthma is three times higher among children today than among their parents. Incidence of eczema is six times higher. An extreme example of chemical pollution in food concerned the early onset of puberty—breast development and growth of pubic hair—in girls under the age of ten in Puerto Rico. They had eaten chicken laced with growth hormones.

*Fifty percent of antibiotics produced in the US are administered to animals.* The repeated small doses of antibiotics that intensively raised animals receive in their food results in virulent strains of antibiotic-resistant bacteria. Research indicates that the immunity, which veal calves, poultry, pigs, and cattle develop to their daily intake of antibiotics, can be passed on to humans. In addition, according to a Centers for Disease Control study on salmonella, "anti-microbial-resistant organisms of animal origin cause serious human illness."

Medical doses of antibiotics given to humans are short and sharp to avoid long-drawn-out treatments during which resistance to particular antibiotics may be acquired. Frequency of exposure rather than dosage seems also to be critical to some of the unwanted and notoriously unpredictable side effects in humans, such as anemia, bleeding from the kidney, obstruction of the flow of urine, etc. Long-term exposure to small doses of antibiotics through the consumption of meat and poultry, in addition to developing resistance to antibiotics, may cause chronic yeast infections, skin lesions, severe allergies, asthma and eczema, and hepatitis among others. Diagnosis is difficult as they appear unrelated to the intake of drug-tainted meat.

What are the consequences of resistance to a drug? Organisms become immune to effects of certain antibiotics and if these organisms infect a human, then those antibiotics don't work, leaving the patient susceptible to extended illness. Secondly, in a natural process known as cross-resistance, one organism may pass on to another unrelated organism its own resistance to a drug or group of drugs; thereafter, those drugs will not affect the second organism either, even though it has had no contact with them.

A small selection of the numerous organisms that can acquire this type of resistance includes typhoid fever (a strain of salmonella), gonorrhea, meningitis, enteric fever, septicemia, abscesses in lungs, liver, and heart.

Through cross-resistance, several strains of salmonella—a common cause of food poisoning—have become highly resistant to such life-saving drugs as penicillin and tetracycline. And as of 1984, 25 percent of salmonella in humans is resistant to multiple drug therapies. The death rate in patients hospitalized for salmonella poisoning is one in thirty-five—and getting higher. The importance of salmonella poisoning as a factor in human health is clearly recognized when a spokesman for the USDA admits on national television that an astonishing 35 percent of poultry on supermarket shelves is contaminated with salmonella bacteria—insidiously making every restaurant and home kitchen a potential breeding ground for serious food poisoning. During the slaughter process, each disemboweled chicken carcass is rinsed in a vat of "fecal soup," soaking up to 12 percent of its sale weight in the salmonella-laced liquid. According to the Director of the Central Public Health Laboratory in London, virtually all frozen poultry in Britain is contaminated with salmonella.

It should be reiterated that as we become more resistant to antibiotics, their effectiveness is less when we really need them. Returning to preantibiotic medicine through our own stupidity is a real possiblity.

What is the purpose of administering large quantities of drugs to factory-farm animals? Are they always sick? Yes. Animals stressed physically and psychologically to the limit by the conditions in factory farms get sick and need medical attention. Secondly, even animals that are not sick are under great pressure and might get whatever the sick ones have—so they are given preventative doses.

Thirdly, small doses of antibiotics, growth hormones, and other drugs are given to stimulate faster growth in animals, in the constant quest for ever-quicker profits. Fourthly, pesticides may be included in the diet to rid the barns and holding pens of flies and other parasites. Some of these pesticides are designed to pass through the animal and kill insect larvae hatching in the manure.

Clearly, antibiotics and other drugs are not used to further the well-being of the animals—it is a question of money. Drugs are merely a tool the factory farmer cynically uses to churn out faster and fatter animals who can still manage to walk to their deaths. This tool increases efficiency and revenue for the farmer by reducing the numbers of animals that succumb to the appalling conditions of life on the factory farm, and therefore it helps to keep down the price of meat at the supermarket counter. This shortsighted policy saves a few dollars off the grocery bill, but it guarantees far greater long-term costs in human medical care, disease, pain, and discomfort, from the unknown potential effects of repeated small doses of these drugs on the people who eat the meat.

Antibiotics not only kill off the "bad" organisms—if these are not already resistant—but also the "good" organisms that aid the animal's immune system and protect against disease. By killing off the good with the bad, the animals are actually left more susceptible to disease. And, in fact, factory-farm animals dosed regularly with antibiotics are not necessarily intrinsically healthy animals—the obvious clinical symptoms of disease just don't show.

As a British veterinarian summed it up, unhappy at the direction his profession was taking, "Once vets were people who looked after the well-being of animals, both farm and domestic. But now, we just suppress the disease until it's time for the animal to be killed."

A list of the thousands of drugs, medications, stimulants, and hormones involved includes the familiar penicillin, tetracycline, and other antibiotics; various sulpha drugs such as sulfaquinoxaline and nicotine sulfate; growth stimulants some of which have been classified as possible carcinogens, like the still-available diethylstilbestrol (DES); antioxidant preservatives such as BHT and BHA; arsenicals such as "3-Nitro" or arsenilic acid and arsenosobenzine, and a vast number of others.

Feed manufacturers are permitted to include as a regular supplement only so many grams or pounds of these substances per ton of feed and some antibiotics remain under veterinarian control. However, factory-farm operators may buy drugs over the counter and, without veterinary prescription, administer illegal amounts to sick animals as part of regular treatment—or on occasion, shoot up a sickly animal to keep it on its feet for a few hours more till slaughtered. The Food and Drug Administration has warned that one out of every ten calves killed contains illegal levels of drug residue. A consumer eating that part of the animal where medication is concentrated following a recent injection of drugs, may get a number of unpleasant symptoms, among which could be blurred vision, depression, or worse, kidney failure.

Since animal excrement (especially chicken manure) is being re-processed and fed back to chickens, cattle, and other animals—for up to 50 percent of their total intake of food—the drug, hormone, and pesticide additives in the food are becoming more and more concentrated. Furthermore, the recycling of slaughterhouse wastes into animal feeds also increases eventual human consumption of these chemical and other potentially carcinogenic residues, higher levels of cholesterol, and possibly cancer viruses.

Are there no checks to ensure that meat reaching the consumer is of the highest quality? To be sure, USDA inspectors check the quality of slaughtered animals, but there are two major drawbacks to the system. First, inspectors have no time to check each carcass thoroughly. At a chicken slaughterhouse, for instance, an inspector has no more than two seconds to look for cancer and other disease in the heart, lungs, liver, spleen, kidneys, and skin of each dead and plucked chicken as it whizzes by on the conveyor belt. He has time to condemn the insufficiently bled or the bruised bird, but the hidden hazards of drug, insecticide, and other chemical residues cannot be detected by the naked eye.

Second, if there is any doubt about the quality of the meat, samples are taken and sent to a lab for examination. Checking for residues is done on a random basis and then only for certain chemicals. Samples are sent to commercial laboratories for testing, but, as some USDA inspectors have stated, by the time results are received, the chicken has probably already been eaten.

In "large animal" slaughterhouses, inspectors have more time per animal—about one minute—but the inadequate testing process for questionable meat is the same. Inspectors are also under some pressure from the management and employees of the slaughterhouse, with whom they must work every day. When an inspector stops the line to check a carcass or reject it for poor quality everybody waits and loses money. Many inspectors have attested to the laxness inherent in the inspection procedure.

What you see is not always what you get; and the image is often more important than the truth. Factory-produced meat is a typical example; a steak may appear healthy, but the contaminated drug residues remain unseen—and perhaps untasted. In the case of this food, the outcome of the cynical feeding of additives to incarcerated animals to counter their immediate sickness, stress, and suffering is the delayed sickness, pain, and suffering of millions of men and women in this country and around the world.

> . . . A universe is, indeed, to be pitied whose dominating inhabitants are so unconscious and so ethically embryonic that they make life a commodity, mercy a disease, and systematic massacre a pastime and a profession.
>
> Professor J. Howard Moore,
> Better World Philosophy

## A Word about Milk

The dairy industry, faced with overflowing "lakes" of surplus milk, cheese, butter, and other dairy products, is pushing for higher consumption with new products and heavy advertising—"milk does a body good!"? Milk is touted as a healthful, essential food, containing both calcium and protein. Certainly it is good for calves, but is it good for humans?

A cow's milk is designed by nature to turn a forty-five-pound calf into a five-hundred-pound cow; to nourish a simple-witted, small-brained, big-boned creature. It is not intended for more delicately constructed humans with very different characteristics; the composition of human milk and cow's milk tells the story.

Both have similar amounts of calories and fat, but cow's milk has nearly four times the protein and over three times the calcium. On the other hand, human milk has fifteen times the iron, one-and-a-half times the vitamin A, and nearly two-and-a-half times the vitamin C. Clearly, cow's milk is for calves who need to build massive muscle and quickly grow strong bodies, and not for humans who grow physically more slowly while their brains develop the ability to master the complexities of human endeavor. The obvious comparison: an eleven-month-old calf is considered full grown and ready for slaughter, while an eleven-month-old child is still in diapers and can barely walk.

But humans also need calcium and protein, and isn't milk a good source? Possibly in small quantities, but, as medical research has discovered, "increased incidence of heart attacks in the US exactly follows the increased use of homogenized milk." The homogenization process encapsulates the enzyme xanthine oxydase in fat globules, protecting it from digestive enzymes. Instead of being neutralized by stomach acids, the xanthine oxydase passes through the intestine wall into the blood supply and is deposited on the artery lining, contributing to plaque buildup.

When protein and fat consumption are high, the human body cannot process and absorb calcium. And so in the typical Western diet, calcium is urinated out of the body and absorption is decreased. Calcium needs are therefore high to compensate for this loss. The reverse is also true. This is the reason the World Health Organization of the United Nations can recommend a 400-mg daily allowance of calcium for most of the world, while the US, with its high protein/fat diet, recommends twice as much.

The dairy industry nevertheless continues to extol milk as a good source of calcium, especially for those suffering calcium deficiency diseases like osteoporosis. But milk is also high in protein and fat, and so the body cannot use all the calcium. Drinking milk to avoid osteoporosis is like eating candy to lose weight.

Cow's milk holds other problems for humans. Drug and pesticide additives in the cow's diet may be passed on to the consumer, and children drinking milk from bovine growth hormone (BST)–dosed cows may be susceptible to the onset of premature puberty. Pasteurization, intended to destroy bacteria, makes unclean milk clean. As one dairy industry figure put it, "Millions of gallons of milk are sold every day that wouldn't be fit to be drunk if it weren't for pasteurization." And medical doctors who advise their patients to stop drinking milk see health improvements such as increased mental clarity, the end of endless colds and runny noses, and the disappearance of allergies to such common items as dust, cats, and pollen.

Almost 80 percent of the world's population, especially from black, Hispanic, and Asian ethnic groups, does not, after early childhood, produce enough lactase—an enzyme necessary to break down the lactose content of cow's milk—to digest a normal serving of dairy products. Symptoms of lactose intolerance—commonly attributed to other causes—include diarrhea, nausea, cramps, vomiting, and abdominal pain. All these problems with milk are hardly surprising since humans are the only animals to drink milk after childhood or to drink the milk of other species.

# Conclusion

There are acknowledged connections between cigarette smoking and lung cancer, and governments around the world have taken steps, if not to ban smoking, at least to warn the public of the dangers of using tobacco. It seems clear that there are also compelling statistical connections between the consumption of food derived from animals (beef, pork, poultry, specialty or cured meats, and dairy products) and the most common and devastating killer diseases of the modern era (cancer, heart disease, stroke, and diabetes).

And yet instead of clarifying this connection, emphasizing prevention by eliminating the likely culprits from the diet, and taking a public stand against the eating of meat on medical grounds, governments and the body of relevant scientists have so far remained mute, bolstered by traditional food philosophy—actually a far cry from the diet of our great-grandfathers—their own stomachs' lifelong habits and cravings, and the political power and monetary influence of the meat industry and its agribusiness supporters.

Can it be that McDonald's and the steak sizzling on the backyard barbeque—those two important components of the American dream and symbols of the twentieth-century paradigm to which less-developed countries aspire—are seriously endangering the health of the US and the industrialized world? Is it not bizarre that billions of dollars are spent each year producing meat of questionable quality—which is known to contain drug residues, cancerous portions, and bacterial contamination; that this meat is consumed in excessive-enough quantities to produce millions of cases of fatal cancer, heart disease, stroke, diabetes, and other debilitating diseases; that these diseases must be treated at the cost of further billions of dollars of doctors' time, surgical procedures, drugs, related medical research with abused animals, disability allowances, hospital fees—the list is endless; and that the final result of this expense and pain is the untimely death of those unwittingly diseased millions? And all for what? To satisfy some queer and devastatingly misguided notion, based on ancestral habit and phony modern machismo, that man must hunt and kill—or at least eat—dead animals to prove himself strong? Or is it for the ephemeral titillation of a few taste buds on the end of his tongue?

# 9

## Designer Animals and Other Abuse

Many varied research and development institutions support the agri-businessman in his constant search for ways to improve the efficiency, productivity, and profitability of his animal-raising operations. This R & D concerns the manipulation of farm animals; it is separate from the millions of experimental animals "used"—in other words, maimed, addicted, electrocuted, burned, irradiated, wounded, shot, poisoned, drugged, and generally tortured—each year in laboratories around the world (in the US alone, the figure is close to one hundred million). There is no room here to address these animals. Many books already deal with their plight.

Equipment manufacturers offer the factory farmer high-tech and labor-saving machinery. Feed and drug companies provide new nutritional formulas and chemicals that stimulate ever-faster growth and fight the ever-present threat of widespread disease. Government and university laboratories help in both the above fields of research. They also spend tax dollars seeking, through genetic manipulation, to develop mutant animals who will be more productive and more amenable to factory farming, who will fit the meat industry's marketing program—and who will almost prefer a crowded, noisy steel cage to the open green field.

Traditionally, farmers always bred the best of their stock to maintain and improve the quality of the herd or flock. They sought strong, versatile animals who would do well in their part of the world and who would stay healthy. But now, the trend is away from the traditional hardy animal. New breeds and crossbreeds have been developed to meet specific marketing demands, and as these hybrids become popular, the wide variety of traditional breeds is diminishing—many have disappeared. Factory animals—in other words, most of the pigs, dairy cows, beef cattle, and chickens on US farms—are genetically engi-

121

neered, selectively bred, and synthetic to the point of being mere milk-, meat-, or egg-producing machines.

> *The moral duty of man consists of imitating the moral goodness and beneficence of God manifested in the creation toward all his creatures. Everything of persecution and revenge between man and man, and everything of cruelty to animals, is a violation of moral duty.*
>
> Thomas Paine, *The Age of Reason*

Among pigs in the US, nearly all those on factory farms are hybrids of just three traditional breeds—Yorkshire, Hampshire, and Duroc. Many breeds, like the Berkshire and Poland China pigs once found on countless small farms, are now on the list of rare and dwindling domestic animal species.

Several hundred distinct breeds of traditional, all-purpose farmyard hens once existed, but now fewer than a dozen remain outside of zoos and preservation schemes. All commercial poultry stock—broilers, layers, and turkeys—are crossbred. Purebreds are no longer available. The major genetic resources of the world's poultry are now controlled by just nine "primary breeder" companies—most are subsidiaries of multinational corporations—who raise commercial laying stock from three- and four-way crosses. The common ancestry and gene base of these chickens could lead to genetically induced disease epidemics of devastating proportions. If one of the nine goes out of business, what happens to its gene stock?

Gone are the days of breeds of cattle like the South Devon, which provided both milk and beef. The favorite US dairy cow is now the Holstein. Once famous and popular breeds like the Guernsey and Jersey have richer, creamier milk, but Holsteins have a higher yield— and quantity, in factory-farm philosophy, is all that counts.

Male Holsteins are raised for beef and veal, but specialized beef cattle, like the white-face Herefords, Aberdeen Angus, and Charolais among other breeds which supply the more expensive cuts of meat— but no milk—are a very different conformation from dairy cows. The new beef cattle are hurried from birth to death in eleven months—one-third the time of their ancestors.

Each variation has been refined for maximum production in its field, but still the quest for greater and more convenient production continues. As Mason and Singer note in their book *Animal Factories,* "animal scientists use computers to search for more profitable genes and work with sex control, cloning, somatic cell hybridization, gene grafting, and gene transfer in attempts to build souped-up commercial strains of animals." In other words, if the natural creature does not grow the way you want it to, you just trim it, cut it, and adjust it till you get what you want. But at what cost? Who cares what suffering is involved? Here are just a few sample results of modern animal husbandry.

Broiler hens now have meatier bodies than egg-layers—but, through genetic manipulation, they are so top-heavy they can barely walk without falling over. Egg-layers lay more eggs than their forebears. Forty years ago, the average hen laid 100–120 eggs a year; today, her descendants lay more than twice as many. But, after just one year in the cages, they are worn out—"spent"—and good only for soup.

Rate of weight gain has also been increased in pigs, but the traditional legs are often too weak to carry the heavy, redesigned bodies. Lameness and leg deformities are common—over 50 percent of pigs are lame when they go to slaughter.

Sows have been developed that produce larger than normal litters and have more teats, but they were unable to feed all their piglets because the extra teats didn't work.

In Europe, dairy cows are bred to Belgian Blue bulls to produce a more profitable fattening calf, but the result is that most cows cannot give birth without assistance and more frequently need caesarians.

Milk production per cow has more than doubled since the end of World War II—and now new drugs can increase milk flow by a further 40 percent. That's a 180 percent gain in output in forty years. What does this mean to a gentle creature like the cow? No longer are cows the placid animals of the children's book farmyard; the dairy "super" cow is nervous and hyperactive. Her body works continuously at peak and she produces much more milk than her forebears, but her huge and distended udder causes her great discomfort—and she can't wait to be milked. She may even be fitted with a "bra" to protect the udder from being cut and bruised by her own hind feet or from dragging on the dung-covered holding pen.

The arrogant genetic redesigning of nature callously ignores the many generations of misery for those animals—both experimental and production—who suffer with bodies unnaturally altered not for their own evolutionary benefit but merely to satisfy the greed lurking in man's pocket and in his stomach. What good, for instance, has man reaped from the transplanting of a goat's udder from its natural position to its neck? And what of the discomfort of chickens bred to have no feathers, for use in hot climates and to save processing costs? What kind of arrogance is it to splice together embryos of different species to create "geeps"—half sheep, half goat—an experiment already performed at Cambridge University in England and the University of California at Davis?

The objective is to create genetic variations of major farm animals that can be patented. Patenting an animal that is much more productive than its natural kin will bring profits and agricultural power. Every farmer who wants to raise this genetically engineered hybrid will have to pay licensing fees. But what does this mean for the integrity of the animal species? And how far will this process go? The patentability of genetic characteristics is presently restricted in the US to nonhuman "higher life forms"—but, according to a spokesperson from the US Patent Office quoted in the *New York Times,* "it could be extrapolated to human beings."

*Animal factories are one more sign of the extent to which our technological capacities have advanced faster than our ethics. We plow under habitats of other animals to grow hybrid corn that fattens our genetically engineered animals for slaughter. We make free species extinct and domestic species into biomachines. We build cruelty into our diet.*

Jim Mason and Peter Singer, *Animal Factories*

Developing monstrous animals over twice their present and normal size—by injecting, among other procedures, *human* growth genes into the embryos—will not feed the world. The twelve-foot-long pigs and 10,000-pound cattle—now on the drawing boards, so to speak—will just consume more of our already-scarce nonrenewable natural resources, as we shall see in the next chapter. Leaner and faster-growing pigs already developed with human growth gene implants at the USDA research station in Maryland had eye problems, severe arthritis, and were very susceptible to disease. And how close to cannibalism is it to eat bacon grown with human growth genes?

By attempting to create the perfect combination of highly productive but disease-free animals, biotechnology may be set to revitalize animal agriculture. But biotechnology deliberately plows through the over-turns the natural genetic laws that prevent breeding between species. Embryo manipulation and gene transfer make the presumption that animals have no inherent nature, no unique set of needs and interests, no evolutionary purpose of their own. They assume, on the contrary, that animals are here exclusively for man's service, for him to fiddle with as he wishes, and for him to use as building blocks for any Frankensteinian factory-farm monster he may be capable of creating. There is surely an ethical difference between the traditional farmer's selection of the best stock for natural breeding, and the high-tech manipulation of genetic information and invasive microsurgical embryology that deliberately attempts to override nature's genetic limits. Since the compassionate exercise of power over life and death for the billions of animals already alive is a responsibility man has not yet learned to master, can we trust him to play God with the animal kingdom and create new life-forms for his own profit?

*We now live in a world of Salmonella-tainted chickens, Listeria-covered cheese, and beefburgers laced with estrogenic hormones and residues of potent antibiotics. There are very good reasons why people would want to obtain their daily nourishment without pouring fatty and contaminated meat and dairy products through their bloodstream every few hours.*

Michael Klaper, MD

# THE GOLDEN RULE

People have got to understand that the commandment, "Do unto others as you would that they should do unto you" applies to animals, plants, and things as well as to people. It seems to me that if we are to have a better policy towards Nature, we must also have a better philosophy.

Aldous Huxley

The establishment of the common origin of all species logically involves a readjustment of altruistic morals, by enlarging the application of what has been called the Golden Rule from the area of mere mankind to that of the whole animal kingdom.

Thomas Hardy

Christianity:
All things whatsoever ye would that men should do to you, do ye even so unto them: for this is the law and the prophets.

St. Matthew 7:12

Buddhism:
Hurt not others with that which pains yourself.

Udnavarga

Hinduism:
This is the sum of duty: do naught to others which if done to thee, would cause thee pain.

Mahabharata

Islam:
Treat others as thou wouldst be treated. What thou likest not for thyself, dispense not to others.

Sufism—Abdullah Ansari

Jainism:
In happiness and suffering, in joy and grief, we should regard all creatures as we regard our own self, and should therefore refrain from inflicting upon others such injury as would appear undesirable to us if inflicted upon ourselves.

Yogashastra

Judaism:
Whatever is hateful unto thee, do it not unto thy fellow. This is the whole Torah, the rest is explanation.

Rabbi Hillel, First Century B.C.

# 10

# General Outlook on the Environment

The raising of animals for food is directly connected to some of our most pressing concerns about world hunger and the deterioration of the environment—water shortages and pollution, soil erosion and desertification, energy shortages, and the destruction of rain forest.

Not that we are producing too few animals to feed the hungry—quite the opposite. Or that deteriorating environmental conditions make raising animals more costly and difficult—true in some areas, but not the primary problem. Simply put, the increasingly intensive rearing of animals for food on a global scale uses crops and grain products that otherwise could help feed hungry people; it is also a clearly defined cause of the degradation of our natural world. And our everyday food choices in the supermarket help determine the speed and the course of the gloomy environmental prospects for the future.

> *In the relations of man with the animals, with the flowers, with all the objects of creation, there is a whole great ethic [toute une grande morale] scarcely seen as yet, but which will eventually break through into the light and be the corollary and the complement to human ethics.*
>
> Victor Hugo, *Alpes et Pyrenees*

Full blame clearly cannot be placed at the door of factory farming alone; other facets of creeping civilization, industrialization, and the swelling population play major roles. But historically food animals raised by man—whether by modern, traditional, or ancient methods—have left the environment poorer for their presence.

Whether reared for commercial gain, for the wealth that sheer numbers of animals confer on their owners in some societies, or as a hedge against drought, war, or other disaster, food animals are usually stocked in larger numbers than the land can bear. When local resources are exhausted, the animals must be moved to fresh land or food must be imported for them. Either way, as we shall see, they are net consumers of resources.

The negative impact of domestic animals on our total environment is too often overlooked or is accepted as necessary for the existence of man: a proposition that is true only when there are no food alternatives to meat. Yet, in a world of diminishing natural resources, we cannot afford to waste unnecessarily what still remains; we need to take a fresh look at what we eat and how much it really costs.

Facts and figures abound that define the present state of the environment: annual rainfall figures; rates of encroaching desertification and rain-forest destruction; levels of air and water pollution; climatic changes; crop yields in one country; grain exports from another; overpopulation; acres under irrigation; destruction of wildlife habitat; figures for annual consumption per person of meat, fossil fuels, grains, water, etc.; concentration of land ownership; and many more. But from this jumble of information certain trends become clear.

The condition of our environment is worsening faster than efforts to repair it can be effective; the accelerating world population is putting tremendous pressure on present food supplies; natural resources around the world, which in the past have provided us with fresh air, clean water, and the means to grow food, are becoming scarce and spoiled; hunger is widespread—and raising billions of animals in factory farms is making matters much worse.

These statements sound like wild rumors when we look out on the hustle and bustle of Western city life with plenty of everything available at our fingertips and overflowing supermarkets at every corner. But even in a society preoccupied with fancy restaurants, sports, and flashy cars, reports of impending global devastation are increasingly incontrovertible as newspapers, books, think tanks, and concerned organizations bombard us with bad news about the state of our planet. The comfortable air-conditioned goldfish bowl that insulates us from the hard reality of life for most of the world's people is beginning to crack. Sometimes the message is greeted with bemused helplessness, or maybe a check, but too often the reaction is indifference or numb disbelief.

The implications of the loss of our necessary and life-supporting resources on a global scale are apparently not sufficiently understood or urgently enough felt to cause individuals and nations to act promptly and in unison to reverse the process. Yet it is now that moves must be made to avert the otherwise-inevitable conclusion. The collision course is already set, even though point of impact still seems quite some time away and no radical changes are seen from year to year. There is still a belief that breakthroughs in technology will always find the right solutions when the time comes, and that man can somehow do without the gifts, splendors, and riches of nature.

For our purposes here, two questions need addressing: first, what is the condition of these resources and how long before they are exhausted?; and second, how have animals raised for food contributed to the problem?

This chapter gives only a brief insight into the situation—a full discussion would need another book. But before addressing the state of the resources we must take a quick look at the second question.

## What Have Animals to Do with It?

Domestic animals, both grain-fed in factory farms and grazing out on open pasture, are part of the complex environmental problem because they eat—and they eat in great quantity.

Much of the world's prime agricultural land—in the US over 90 percent of total agricultural land—is used to grow food for animals. Meanwhile, billions of human beings are deprived of a decent diet, because Western and industrialized countries can pay more for grain to feed their animals than poorer nations can pay for grain to feed their citizens. Worldwide, 600 million tons of grain are fed to livestock annually—40 percent of total world grain production.

In nature animals eat what they can get. The weak die, the fit survive, and predators keep the numbers in check. Seldom do wild animals destroy the food supply of their habitat—unless under pressure from the encroaching influence of man.

But forced to multiply, reared in huge numbers by humans, protected from predators and encouraged to get fat, domestic animals eat more than a fair share. And they eat everything—from dry grasses and scrub on semi-desert rangeland to the high-quality grains and legumes grown especially for them. The deterioration, erosion, and desertification of range and pasture land puts increased pressure on croplands to provide animal feeds—thereby, as *The State of the World 1990* notes, "intensifying the competition between humans and animals for scarce food supplies."

Factory-farming systems are voracious users of these grains to stimulate productivity and to fatten the animals quickly, but their supply, which represents only a cash expense to the factory farmers, generates life-threatening and very real long-term, short-term, and immediate costs for everybody else on the planet.

While factory farms are a concentrated cause of environmental degradation, rangeland pasturing and nomadic herding—and most other methods of animal husbandry—also bear direct responsibility because of the huge numbers of animals involved, even though their effect is more scattered.

It is often argued that the land used for grazing animals is usually not suitable for other agricultural purposes, and that raising meat is the best and highest use of this land, as far as feeding humans is concerned. Ignoring for a moment the ethical aspects of killing animals to eat them, and the underlying notion that all land has to be used for a human purpose, this position is only sometimes correct. It may be preferable to preserve a watershed to benefit a whole region, to preserve wild strains of food crops and maintain genetic diversity, or to protect rain-forest land with its vast potential of medicinal plants. Grazing is only acceptable if the stocking density of animals is kept realistically proportionate to the ecological soundness of the land—so that the effect of grazing on the sustainability of the local environment is scarcely more than that of passing wildlife.

*To live compassionately and with conscience, in reverence of all life, is the spiritual transformation that the humane, animal rights and "deep" ecology movements are helping bring about. Making compassion an integral part of the life-style of the 80s is an auspicious beginning for the millennium to come.*

Dr. Michael W. Fox

But large roaming herds of sheep, goats, and cattle eat back and trample grass and other vegetation to the point that the natural feed is exhausted, the natural water cycle is disrupted, and the plant life cannot recover. Historically, pastureland has always been overstocked and overgrazed. And desertification, climate changes, erosion, flooding, and famine have often followed. This scenario is especially common in arid and semi-arid areas around the world. A classic example is the land surrounding the Mediterranean, once thickly forested and lush, now barren and dry from thousands of years of overgrazing.

# How Long?

Seventeenth-century British philosopher Francis Bacon wrote, "Nature, to be commanded, must be obeyed," but industrialized man, to satisfy greed and hunger, has only tried to command. He has looked on the world anthropocentrically, as though he were the only important life-form, taking what he wanted and giving little in return. He has not understood the principle of coexistence and the benefit of mutual regard. He has not learned how to obey the laws of nature and therefore he has not learned how to make for himself a permanent and sustainable home. He is perpetually at the edge of crisis with nature.

In the past, man's numbers were small and so was his long-term impact. Now, a rapidly growing population has at its disposal powerful technology. Even as he tries to extract the maximum food and wealth from the natural world, he is destroying it in vast measure. The onslaught is deliberate, and in our lifetimes, possibly irreversible.

Fortunately, there is also a growing awareness and understanding of the damage already done, a desire to violate no longer the processes of nature, and a willingness to change life-styles in order to create a lasting cooperative relationship.

This is just as well, for human labor, effort, and ingenuity are some of the few immediately renewable resources. Most of the other resources—including those used in raising animals—are finite or may only renew themselves over the very long term.

# Water

About 100 thousand cubic miles (420,000 km³) of water falls on the earth each year as rain and snow. Yet despite this annual deluge, there is a global water shortage.

Around the world in arid and semi-desert areas crops are failing because of bad land management and changing rainfall patterns that are often directly attributable to deforestation for grazing and other purposes. Other areas are flooding, but the water cannot be used or saved. Even in temperate climates, rainfall is not enough to meet agricultural needs, and big cities with their many inhabitants and industries consume so much water they must pipe it in from hundreds of miles around, permanently drawing down natural reservoirs, water tables, and lakes, and reducing the amount available for local agriculture.

But what has this water use to do with raising animals for food, other than the fact that the animals drink water every day? It is quite simple: the high protein grains fed to animals need huge amounts of water to grow. Direct rainfall provides much of this water, but in marginal rainfall areas cropland must be irrigated.

Water from dams, rivers, and lakes cannot supply all the productive but thirsty irrigated areas; a critical amount of irrigation water is "mined" from deep wells that penetrate the aquifer. "Water mining" is an irreversible process because the water is pumped out of the ground, used up, and cannot be replaced by rainfall.

Levels of natural underground water storage are falling. Rainfall cannot replenish the underground aquifers as fast as they are being depleted, because they have been built up over many millions of years and because today the often-poor quality of the topsoil and lack of adequate vegetation prevent the rain from soaking in. Instead, rain runs off taking with it some of the bankrupt but still precious topsoil. In warm areas, even rain that is absorbed evaporates later because of lack of enough ground cover.

In the US, for instance, the Ogallala Aquifer, a vast natural underground reservoir of thousands of square miles stretching from western Texas to Nebraska, was estimated in 1961 to be already depleted by 20 percent. In 1981, it was expected to last only another forty years.

In addition to straightforward water shortages, repercussions from falling groundwater levels include earth subsidence—for example the well-publicized "sinkholes" in Florida—and, more seriously, unexpected and unpredictable seismological activity.

But can animals really eat so much grain that their food affects the supply of water and underground water tables? A US example runs like this: 80 percent of all irrigated cropland is in the seventeen western states and includes 85 percent of the land in the US devoted to growing wheat, barley, and sorghum. These crops depend heavily on irrigation, and billions of gallons of water are pumped out of the ground —although more than 50 percent evaporates, without benefiting the crops. Of all water used in these states, *85 percent goes to irrigation.*

The result is huge quantities of grains. After exports—which account for some 30 percent of the West's farm earnings—the US produces nearly 2,900 pounds (about 1,300 kg) of grains per person per year. But the bottom line is this: *of those 2,900 pounds, only 20 percent is eaten directly by humans; animals eat the rest*—cattle on feedlots, broilers, egg-layers, etc. The story is similar in the Midwest where vast acreages of corn are fed to pigs. To compound this squandering of land, water, energy, and food, more than half the grain exported from the US to other countries goes to fatten their animals, not to feed their people.

The water used to grow the animals' grain, combined with their drinking needs and the water used in processing their carcasses, amounts to some 2,500 gallons per day for each person in the US who eats meat. This figure represents food production use only, and does not include household needs and the per capita share of other industrial consumption. In contrast, one who eats no meat accounts for no more than 300 gallons per day for his food.

Clearly, the growing of these grains simply to feed animals is contributing to the depletion of the aquifers and accelerating future global water shortages. And here is the major concern; if we use up irreplaceable ground water now, what unknown legacy are we leaving to our children? What is the long-term cost?

# Water Pollution

A typical pig producer with two thousand animals must deal with twenty-seven tons of manure and thirty-two tons of urine every week. And an egg factory with sixty thousand caged layer hens produces over eighty tons of manure every week—and there are some 350 million layer hens in the US. In all, farm animals in the US create about 2 billion tons of manure each year, about ten times the amount produced by humans.

This huge quantity of waste could be recycled as fertilizer or used for methane gas production, if properly managed. Proper waste treatment would extract or neutralize the unwanted, but potent mix of nitrates, phosphates, drug residues, and other chemicals in the feces, the result of factory-farm animals' unnatural and concentrated diet. But most operators consider the manure as simply a waste product. Most of it is left untreated and allowed to wash freely into streams, rivers, lakes, and other waterways.

A further and more massive leaching of chemicals into the groundwater comes from the heavy applications throughout the year of powerful fertilizers, insecticides, and herbicides on the depleted cropland soils, where feed grains are grown. This combination adds up to a destructive pollutant of water both above and below ground.

Lakes and streams become "dead" and begin to stink because natural chemical reactions that neutralize the nitrates and phosphates take up large amounts of oxygen out of the water. Polluted water therefore has a reduced oxygen content, and fish and other water dwellers that need oxygen can no longer survive. In the US, contaminated aquifers are also permanently ruining thousands of household wells, and generally affecting the ability to obtain drinkable water.*

So not only do factory-farm animals consume precious water in growing their food, they cause heavy pollution of remaining water supplies with the vast tonnage of their toxic body wastes. Factory farming further pollutes when the animals are killed; enormous quantities of waste water are produced in the killing and packing process. A single small chicken-slaughtering and processing plant, for instance, may use 100 million gallons of water daily, enough to service a community of twenty-five thousand people.

*The obligations of law and equity reach only to mankind; but kindness and beneficence should be extended to the creatures of every species, and these will flow from the breast of a true man, as streams that issue from the living fountain.*

Plutarch

## Soil Quality

Nearly 90 percent of US cropland is devoted to growing feeds for livestock. The pressure of maximizing crop production and minimizing costs has led the farmer to practices that are destroying his land. Short-term goals are being met, but the continuous forced growing of grains and other feed crops greatly harms the quality of the soil—and more and more chemical fertilizers, weed-killers, and pesticides are required to get the crops out of the ground. Since 1960, crop output per unit of chemical input has decreased by 50 percent and it is still falling.

Over many years this shortsighted land management has left the topsoil prone to erosion from wind, dust storms, and especially runoff after heavy rains. Topsoil regenerates at rates dependent on type and

---

*A 1990 government study on the environment reported groundwater in twenty-six states contaminated by forty-six identifiable pesticides from agricultural run-off.

use of the land; in the US, an optimistic general figure for cropland renewal is five tons per acre per year. But, since average annual cropland topsoil is eroding at twelve tons/acre/year, there is a net loss.

Worldwide, valuable cropland topsoils are eroding and washing away down rivers faster than natural replacement. According to a report by the European Parliament's committee on the environment, modern industrial farming techniques are despoiling the European ecology; in Britain, nearly 40 percent of farmland is subject to a dangerous rate of erosion.

But prudent soil management practices that can halt erosion cost too much and mean reduced output per acre. Operators have been more concerned with meeting today's bills than with the future agricultural viability of their land.

Rangeland is also deteriorating worldwide because of the pressure of overgrazing. Clear examples of this destruction are in Australia where early settlers ringbarked and killed millions of trees to "improve" rangeland pasture. In the two hundred years since Europeans arrived and began grazing their vast herds of sheep and cattle, half the topsoil has gone.* In the Southwestern states of the US, where heavy overgrazing on state and federal "public grazing lands" has left permanent damage, there are millions of acres of barren wasteland where once there was luxuriant vegetation.

Traditional herdsmen keep on the move in order to preserve their pastures for the next visit. But even so, their sheep, goats, and cattle have overgrazed pasture, kept normal vegetation below its potential, and left the soil prone to erosion. Too many animals stay on too small an area for too long, and herders, either deliberately or through ignorance, have not put enough effort and money back into nurturing the land.

Historical and present-day evidence indicates that, especially in hotter, dryer climates, domestic animals kept by humans have been and still are the major cause of worldwide desertification. Extreme results are seen today in the Sahel region of Central Africa, where fertile land weakened by poor rainfall has become desert. Lower rainfall may follow from heavy overgrazing and reduced vegetation, since, according to some climatologists, vegetation and rainfall are interdependent. Clearing unsuitable land for agriculture and cutting trees for firewood are two other shortsighted land-management practices that lead to desertification.

Within the US, foraging domestic animals even now are destroying temperate forests and wooded areas as the quality of existing range-

---

*In 1989, Australia announced a plan to plant 1 billion trees during the 1990s.

land deteriorates. Two-thirds of the forest land lost between 1967 and 1975 became grazing land.

In the US, Department of Agriculture figures show 2 billion tons of rangeland topsoil lost each year. The Department of the Interior names grazing—after agriculture—as the second major cause of soil loss and damage; 60 percent of US rangelands are seriously overgrazed. The Bureau of Land Management conservatively states 40 percent of its land is seriously eroded. Millions of acres are being trampled into wasteland; topsoil is washing away, soil fertility is decreasing, springs and creeks are going dry, water tables are dropping, and native animal and plant wildlife are disappearing.

Reducing the intensity of grazing can bring an effective halt to rangeland erosion—though damaged land will take years to recover—but operators everywhere are under pressure to produce competitive feeds and animals. Fewer animals on the range mean more expensive meat and less money for the ranchers.

In addition to future real costs, there are current monetary expenses. Public lands used for grazing in the US are costing the government ten times more money to manage and to recover from overgrazing than the pittance being received in lease payments. Effectively, this amounts to a federal subsidy for ranchers. Government is spending hundreds of millions of dollars for rangeland improvements; unfortunately, these improvements mean modifying the scarce water resources and natural ecosystems for further profit—in other words, for cattle—not reinstating their original beauty and natural order.

Not only have domestic grazing animals reduced lush vegetation to wasteland, they have been responsible—actually their keepers, of course—for the mass slaughter of other animals, both predators and competitors for the rangeland grasses. Coyotes, wolves, dingoes, foxes, bears, large cats like mountain lions and leopards, small cats like bobcats and lynx, deer, elk, kangaroos, wild sheep, wild horses and asses, and many, many other species, large and small, have been killed off by the millions to protect domestic animals and their feed, putting many of these wild animals on the endangered species list. It is especially appalling that so much of this killing to protect private herds occurs on public lands.

*Compassion . . . can only attain its full breadth and depth if it embraces all living creatures and does not limit itself to mankind.*

Dr. Albert Schweitzer

# The Destruction of Rain Forests

Rain forests and other tropical forest areas are being cut down around the world at the rate of fifty-nine acres a minute—or 31 million acres every year, according to the World Wildlife Fund. That's nearly a football field every second, or an area the size of the US state of New York destroyed each year.

The rain forests are effectively nonrenewable. Some areas have taken sixty million years to become what they are, though some scientists estimate that tropical rain forests could recover from deforestation in a thousand years, provided there were a nearby source of plant and animal species. Since the early fifties the world has lost one-fifth of its rain forests and at the present rate of destruction, there will be no significant areas left in forty years. Nobody knows what effect the complete elimination of tropical forests will have on the planet.

Rain forests support half the different species of flora and fauna that exist on earth, containing between 5–20 million species of plants, insects, and animals, most of which have yet to be catalogued. In clearing tropical rain forests especially, we will lose a vast resource for scientific research into the untapped medicinal and healing properties of the huge varieties of plant life. Rain forests also offer unique wilderness and recreational opportunities.

But most importantly, with their vast and dense accumulation of breathing vegetation, rain forests affect local and global climate and regulate rainfall. The Amazon's forest actually creates by transpiration 50 percent of the rain that falls in that region, but it affects climate for thousands of miles around.

Rain forests also contribute to the stability of the oxygen/carbon dioxide balance in our atmosphere. Slash-and-burn programs of forest destruction release vast quantities of carbon into the air, raising the atmospheric $CO_2$ level and intensifying the "greenhouse effect." One scientific study attributes one quarter of the annual global carbon buildup to deforestation.

In Central and South America and in the band of tropical forests that circle the globe at the equator, giant rain-forest trees and the richly varied vegetation are being hacked down in a story of deliberate, systematic, and unregulated destruction.

Multinational corporations, large landowners, and subsistence peasant farmers, encouraged by government agricultural policies and land grants, are cutting forest for its lumber and to create grazing land for cattle—since 1960, more than a quarter of all Central American forests have been destroyed to produce export beef, which is the chief culprit in *all* Latin-American rain-forest destruction. In some countries, chopping down rain forest on virgin land is considered an "improvement" and is enough to give legal title to it.

In many areas, wood products are only a by-product of the process, because the huge variety of trees—over a hundred different species per acre compared to fewer than ten in temperate forests—makes commercial specialization expensive. It is faster to cut and burn than to sort out and use all the different woods available. Once cleared by bulldozer, the land is burned, then sown with grass seed.

Rain-forest soil can sustain lush forest growth for thousands of years because the rain-forest growth cycle draws up to 95 percent of its nutrients from decomposing vegetation, and as little as 5 percent from the soil. The soil itself is too poor to support cattle for more than three or four years. Once the soil is exhausted, the area is abandoned, more forest is cut down, and the cattle move on.

In Brazilian Amazonia, nearly all ranches cleared before 1978 have now been abandoned. On such ranches, where land is cheap, meat production barely reached forty-five pounds per acre (50 kg per hectare) whereas on high-priced European organic farmland using no imported feeds, meat production can be over five hundred pounds per acre plus around one thousand gallons of milk. These figures reflect the low cost of these wasteful operations in monetary terms, but the incalculable cost is in irreplaceable forest.

In some Central American countries the overall production of beef has increased dramatically in the last twenty-five years—in Costa Rica, production is more than three times the 1961 level. Most of this beef is exported to the US and other Western nations, and consumed in fast-food operations—this imported beef, according to US government figures, lowered the price of a hamburger in the US by five cents. But as exports have climbed, local per capita consumption of beef has actually declined—some countries have been known to ration domestic sales of beef. And so the ancient and noble forests of the world are being devastated by local and multinational corporations in the dubious cause of the cheap hamburger.

*The missing link between animals and a truly humane mankind is man himself, who does not yet see himself as a part of the world, claiming it instead for himself.*

Dr. Michael W. Fox, *One Earth, One Mind*

# Oil and Fossil Fuels

Most people are familiar with the concept of oil shortage; they remember the recent lines of cars at service stations waiting to fill up with scarce fuel. But despite the current availability of gasoline and other oil-based products, worldwide reserves of this commodity are finite, and increasingly difficult and expensive to extract.

Because of the immediate effect upon our lives of a shortage of energy—lines at the pump or power outages just at mealtimes—we are conscious of our precarious dependence on those energy sources needed to drive our equipment, our economy, and, indeed, our lives. And we are aware that this resource cannot last forever. Unfortunately, such an understanding and sense of immediacy does not yet apply to topsoil loss, water pollution, and the destruction of rain forests and other habitats; the loss of these natural resources will be even more grave.

Present energy use in the US for agricultural and food production amounts to approximately 20 percent of all energy used in the US—depending on what is included in the "production" process—and represents per capita more than *twice* the amount spent in many other less-industrialized countries for *all* their energy uses combined.

The factory-farming industry is a net consumer of energy. The production of millions of tons of feed grains requires highly mechanized, fuel-extravagant crop-growing methods; factory-farm efficiency means lots of expensive equipment and automation in animal management; and modern slaughterhouses and processing plants are energy intensive. The result is a poor energy input to food output ratio.

This cost is clearly understood when we see that for every calorie of fossil fuel input we get back from meat products at best only one-quarter (.25) of a calorie of food energy; a broiler hen returns only one-fourteenth (.07) of a calorie, while feedlot beef returns merely .03 food calories—*a ratio of just one food calorie received for every thirty-three fuel calories expended.*

In contrast, for every calorie of fossil fuel input in the energy-intensive US, plant foods (beans, grains, and vegetables) return from 1.25 to 2.5 food calories—*five times as much as meat, and more.* Less-developed countries return higher amounts—up to eighty food calories of plant origin for each calorie of fossil fuel input.

Simply stated, agribusiness methods in the US and other Western countries require that we put more fuel energy into the system than we take out in food energy. Where this negative energy flow presently exists, it cannot last indefinitely; and there are certainly not enough fossil fuel resources available in the world for all countries to operate at the same high level of agricultural energy input.

# World Hunger

The Western world has one and a half times as much to eat per person as the developing countries. Caloric intake in Europe and the US is between 3,300 and 3,700 calories per day per person—in Africa, it is less than 2,300 (this figure is an average and hides the millions who barely subsist). Animal products form over 30 percent of the US diet, while they are less than 7 percent for the average African, and just over 2 percent for someone living in Burundi. These few figures clearly show the huge food imbalance between rich and poor nations.

In no way can resources be produced—or spared—to bring animal food to the table of everyone in the world at the level of today's consumption by Western countries. Even in the industrialized countries, the present level of production of this luxurious food—luxurious in the sense that it is nonessential—is not sustainable because it requires a too-extravagant use of limited raw materials. And the much-touted efficiency and productivity of intensive farming methods evaporates when we realize that the real costs are hidden far away beyond the supermarket meat counter, and borne elsewhere by other people.

An immediate and important result of the demands of modern animal farming on the resources of the planet is the apparent worldwide shortage of food and the plight of the "starving millions." Although politics and the physical distribution of food are major factors in world hunger, the evidence remains clear that the vast tonnage of food fed to animals to supply the rich countries with their heavily meat-based diet is given at the expense of hungry people around the world. According to the United Nations Food and Agricultural Organization, the world now grows enough human edible grain to provide each person on earth with 3,600 calories a day—more than one and a half times the recommended amount in a normal diet.

However, feeding those 600 million tons of grains to animals and raising billions of animals to feed humans is not only a waste of natural resources—an inefficient use of the food value produced and an extreme cruelty to the animals—but it is also callously indifferent to the undernourished people in the world, to the 1/2 billion more, mostly women and children, who are chronically malnourished, and to the 40 thousand children who die of starvation every day. The food given to factory-farm animals depends on the same basics—wheat, soybeans, vitamins, and minerals—as the food needed for famine relief.

Increases in population and the concomitant demand for food have strained resources and made worse the problem of feeding everybody. But while the number of poor grows, added pressure on food resources is coming from the nouveaux riches in industrializing countries and elsewhere who, seeking to emulate the Western style of life, are demanding more and more high primary-food-consuming meat products.

An example of this trend is in Bangladesh, a poor country that must import food grains to feed its people. The recent development of an intensive broiler and egg-laying industry, although minuscule by Western standards, supplies the few wealthy with chicken and eggs but requires extra imports of grains that the country—and the poor—can ill afford.

Third World factory farming dramatically increases demand for food grains and pushes the price out of reach of those in desperate need. In Mexico, according to Oxfam, the international relief organization, 80 percent of children in rural areas are undernourished while livestock—much of which is exported—is fed more grain than the whole human population eats.

If animals put on one pound of weight for every pound of food they ate, there would be no shortage, no net loss of food from the system and the meat available could feed those in need. All we would have to do then would be to distribute the meat fairly and make sure everybody had enough money to buy it. But the food-to-weight-gain ratio of animals—as with humans—is not one to one.

The following table shows the pounds of grain needed to produce one pound of meat and the pounds of grain protein needed to produce one pound of meat protein. (Meat does contain all the essential amino acids that go to make up the protein that human bodies need—and so it should, since the composition of meat so closely resembles that of human flesh. But remember, grains are also an excellent source of protein. They are after all what the animals eat to create protein.)

| Animal | lbs feed/ 1 lb meat | lbs grain protein/ 1 lb meat protein |
|---|---|---|
| Chicken | 3 | 5.5 |
| Pigs | 6 | 8.3 |
| Cattle | 12–16 | 21.4 |

*[Animals] are not brethren; they are not underlings; they are other nations, caught with ourselves in the net of life and time, fellow prisoners of the splendour and travail of the earth.*

Henry Beston, *The Outermost House*

Clearly, not all the specific grains and legumes grown for animals are suitable for normal human diet. For example, the $2.5 million worth of linseed cake, cottonseed cake, and rapeseed meal exported by Ethiopia during the height of the 1985 famine in that country and fed to farm animals in Britain was not edible by people. But by more sensitive management of the quantity of energy used, the fertile cropland available, and the other resources needed to produce and distribute these grains, human hunger could be significantly impacted.

Another twist in the hunger-and-resource story is land ownership. Large tracts of the most fertile and irrigated Third World land are controlled by multinationals—or local groups who know "where the money is"; a study of eighty-three countries shows that a mere 3 percent of landholders own 80 percent of the farmland. Instead of meeting the food and nutrition needs of the people of the area, they grow and export carcass meat, feeds for animals, and moneymaking cash crops like coffee, sugar, flowers, and cocoa—and set the world prices for them. The resulting lack of suitable agricultural land to feed themselves has forced local farmers to cultivate marginal areas, which cannot long support heavy grazing and crop growing, and soon deteriorate into desert and wasteland.

An example of this process is the drought-stricken Sahelian region in central West Africa. Peanut cultivation, forced on the local agricultural communities by foreign commercial interests at the expense of subsistence food crops, later became a critical factor in paying off mounting debts to First World banks. More and more land was taken to grow peanuts to earn foreign exchange, less and less was available for food crops and grazing animals. Farmers and nomads were pushed further into marginal regions and eventually were blamed for overgrazing and encroaching desertification.

The "world food shortage" does not exist; it is essentially a world food imbalance, due to inequitable distribution. As the UN figures for presently available grain calories per day have shown us, the world is now growing enough food for all people to eat well—it is just not going into the right mouths. World food market control, land ownership, and especially politics all combine to determine who gets food and who does not. There is more profit and political mileage to be gained by supplying meat to the rich than by giving grain to the poor.

# Conclusion

Some societies and civilizations, like the Amish in Pennsylvania, have developed over time sustainable animal-farming practices in which the long-term health of the soil and the environment is not sacrificed to short-term excesses. But as farming elsewhere ceases to be an individual's way of life and becomes just another corporate means of making money, making sure natural resources are available tomorrow is a priority only if it helps cash flow today.

The callous factory-farm industry is especially responsible for the selfish squandering of millions of tons of potential human food on animals who become unhealthy, unnecessary, and frequently diseased foods for the rich, while fellow humans elsewhere must make do with not quite enough rice or millet to take away the pain of hunger.

But while domestic animals may be the cause, they are in no way to blame for the state of the environment. Quite the contrary. They may be exhausting our natural resources and chowing down on excessive amounts of food, but they are not the last link in the food chain. This honor belongs to their human keepers who have caused them to procreate in such numbers and consume in such quantities that our natural environment has been put at dire risk. Ultimately, the humans who eat this extravagant meat must bear responsibility, whether they are aware of it or not.

We have the technical skills and enough remaining resources to prevent the complete destruction of our natural environment and also to feed everybody who is hungry. The question is, have we the will to save the planet, the determination to change our life-styles and our way of thinking, and the understanding to recognize that today no part of the earth and no section of our global society can survive for long when all the rest is destroyed?

> *It must be apparent that we cannot go on as we have been. We are killing the earth, killing the animals, killing ourselves—this is the true meaning of Agricide.*
>
> Dr. Michael W. Fox, *Agricide*

44. (Top) This is Felicity, a laying hen just released after two years in a battery cage. Her condition is typical. Despite industry claims that the genetically manipulated and specially bred modern laying hen has no need of a natural environment, and although in poor physical shape, Felicity started pecking and scratching in the grass as soon as her deformed feet would let her.

45. (Bottom) This is Felicity—one year later, with the help of her friends.

# 11

# Is There Another Way?

We have developed a blind spot. Concern mounts for world hunger, for environmental degradation and pollution, for human health, and for drug and chemical residues in our food; all concerns that relate to the impact of factory farming on the community. But the ethical issue of compassion for the gross and inhumane treatment of farm animals themselves is not being addressed. We manage to overlook this violence in our midst, yet the animals bear the greatest cost of the factory-farm system, and there is much ignorance about their lot. Why do we condone their suffering and think of them only as food? Are we reluctant to see them in any other way?

Aboriginal peoples around the world have always recognized the interdependence of all life and know man as an integral part of nature, not its conqueror. Their reverence for the earth's bounty and respect for all life extends even to the animals killed for food, for these are not always taken easily. All forms of food procuring, including the slaying of animals, take place in a spirit of thanks and prayer. They recognize that the animal gives up its life so the hunter may continue his. As a South Sami Lapp woman from northern Sweden put it even today, "Our men care for the (rein)deer and know them. When (rein)deer are slaughtered, it is done with respect." The beliefs of these cultural groups with their distinct, enduring ways of life contrast with those of Western civilized man—the self-important and self-appointed "master" of nature—who believes the world only exists to serve his needs, and who long ago lost his reverence for nonhuman life. "Forget the pig is an animal. Treat him like a machine in a factory. Schedule treatments like you would lubrication. Breeding like the first step in an assembly line. And marketing like the delivery of finished goods," is the attitude expressed in "Raising Pigs by the Calendar," in *Hog Farm Management*, expressing typical factory-farm irreverence for life.

For better or worse, the paradigm of modern civilization—our philosophical prescriptions, our values, and our ethics—is based on the European distillation of ancient Greek philosophy, Judaism, and Christianity. What we believe today, what is considered the norm around the world is heavily influenced by Christian thought—even in the Soviet Union and other Communist countries, where the fundamental moral values are based on the Judeo-Christian ethic. This ethic, through a creeping "Westernization" process, has become a major influence in the farthest reaches of Asia, Africa, and America. Around the world, local and traditional ethics and values have been and are still being thrust aside or modified to accommodate the influx of this European style of civilization, and to allow the indigenous peoples to emulate the Western ideal of material wealth and high consumption.

*The assumption that animals are without rights, and the illusion that our treatment of them has no moral significance, is a positively outrageous example of Western crudity and barbarity. Universal compassion is the only guarantee of morality.*

Arthur Schopenhauer, *On the Basis of Morality*

Philosophically, our attitude towards animals is based on the teachings of a few key interpreters of Christian thought. The Bible itself offers a multitude of conflicting messages, which have predictably produced a multitude of conflicting interpretations. But the early Christian fathers, closer than we are to the spirit of the teachings of Christ, clearly argued against the eating of meat. Clement of Alexandria (A.D. 160–240), founder of the Alexandrian school of theology and greatest Christian apologist of the second century, wrote, "It is far better to be happy than to have our bodies act as graveyards for animals," and St. John Chrysostom (345–407), archbishop of Constantinople, reiterated, "We, the Christian leaders, practice abstinence from the flesh of animals to subdue our bodies. . . . The unnatural eating of flesh is polluting." While they ate no meat, they did not argue strongly for humane treatment of animals as an end in itself, as did the Greek philosopher Pythagoras and Roman writers such as Ovid, Seneca, Porphyry, and Plutarch.

The Middle Ages brought the example and teachings of St. Francis of Assisi who said, "Not to hurt our humble brethren is our first duty to them, but to stop there is not enough. We have a higher mission—to be of service to them wherever they require it." St. Francis's compassionate treatment of animals became famous throughout Europe. Meanwhile, other Christian theologians harked back to Aristotelian theory that the power of the intellect and the power of reason were supreme, and that the physical, sensual side of human nature hindered the performance of these higher functions. Animals, accorded little reasoning power but great preoccupation with their senses and bodily functions, were therefore deemed inferior and imperfect beings.

In particular, the writings of the thirteenth-century Dominican St. Thomas Aquinas exerted great power over Christian theology and morality—as they do to this day. He considered merciful and kind treatment of animals to be valuable only because cruelty towards animals leads to cruelty towards humans. Man had no moral duty to animals for their own sakes and should have no concern for their feelings or sentience—let alone rights. Man could not sin against "irrational animals" because sinning was restricted to sins against God, against oneself, and against one's neighbors.

Aquinas taught that man could only have moral obligations to those who possessed an immortal soul. Irrational animals had no immortal souls, and, therefore, as imperfect creatures, had no moral standing. This teaching is somewhat in contrast to the exact Hebrew words of Genesis 1:30, which describe "beasts of the field" and "fowls of the air" as having "living souls." Animals were not the only beings to suffer from St. Thomas's dictums. At one point he argued that women also had no souls and that therefore man had no moral obligation to them. From today's perspective, Aquinas's views on the possession of souls seem somewhat suspect.

*There can be no double standard. We cannot have peace among men whose hearts find delight in killing any living creature.*

Rachel Carson, *Silent Spring*

In the mid-1600s, the French philosopher René Descartes, a potent influence over the temper of the seventeenth-century rebirth of scientific enquiry, declared that animals were machines put on earth for man's use. Since they were made by "the hands of God," he said, they were more efficient than any machines that man could possibly make, but nevertheless, they were nothing more than unconscious automatons. They were incapable of enjoying thoughts, feelings, or a mental life of any kind, and they could be treated in any manner man wished. Descartes's followers dissected animals alive, maintaining that the animals' expressions of apparent pain—their howls and screams— were merely symptoms of the machine's breaking down.

Descartes's pronouncements about the nature of animals were soon shown to be inaccurate as more investigation into the anatomy and physiology of animals revealed similarities to the human being. The physical parallels between animals and humans suggested that animals, like humans, could indeed suffer pain. English utilitarian philosopher Jeremy Bentham in 1780 reflected a turning point in concern for animal welfare when he wrote, "The question is not Can they reason? nor Can they talk? but Can they suffer?" Bentham was one of the first in modern times to look at the question of animal abuse from the animals' point of view.

During the nineteenth century, parallel to the early stirrings of protest against slavery and child labor, and amid budding interest in the general welfare of less-fortunate members of society, concern for unnecessary and excessive cruelty to animals began to grow. In England, the "baiting" of badgers, dogs, and bulls was outlawed by 1850, as was cockfighting, and bills were introduced—and eventually passed—in the House of Commons to protect horses and livestock from wanton mistreatment. From this legislation emerged the world's first animal welfare organization, The Royal Society for the Protection of Animals.

Charles Darwin, in his book *The Origin of the Species* (1859), proposed that all life-forms had evolved through a process of natural selection, and thereby dealt a severe blow to the orthodox Christian belief that creation was a divine design, with man at the center in the image of God, and figuratively revolving around him and serving him, all the animals, fish, plants, the earth and the planets, and the whole solar system. This creationist, anthropocentric view of nature and the world, which encourages man to use or abuse animals in any manner he sees fit, still has not been laid to rest. And the Catholic Church still regards some of the tenets of St. Thomas Aquinas and Descartes as the generally accepted rationale for man's treatment of animals. As late as the middle of the nineteenth century, Pope Pius IX forbade an animal welfare society in Rome, because its existence would imply that man had a moral duty towards animals.

The tone of civilized man's moral attitude to animals continues to reflect this historical, religious view of animals as man's property, toward whom he has no firm ethical obligations and who have no fundamental rights to life. Meanwhile, the industrial and technological revolutions have introduced an insidious commercial influence that, in conjunction with the religious tradition, now dominates our world-view. Progress, ethics, and values are judged by a materialist yardstick; objects are evaluated in terms of their function, and their ability to further material progress. Objects have no worth in themselves; their value lies only in what can be got out of them, what they can be sold for, or what they can be used for. This perception of the world has been the basis for unlimited experimentation on animals and their various uses as expendable items.

Men—and by extension, animals—are reduced to units of monetary value, their lives reflecting a perception of economic output, rather than any intrinsic value as living beings. Thus a chief executive pulls in a salary of one million dollars a year, while a landless farm worker does not even have enough to eat. Dairy cows are automatically slaughtered when they no longer produce enough milk, while prize bulls of the same species, valued at many thousands of dollars, live for many years in relative comfort. Such an attitude values a barnful of caged layer hens by the selling price of a dozen eggs, rather than by the agony of several thousand tortured chickens.

Nevertheless, the last hundred years have seen a marked change in our attitude to animals. We have introduced into the culture a basic recognition that we should be kind to animals, even though so often we only pay lip service to the idea. We believe that animals should not be treated with wanton cruelty because we know that animals have feelings and suffer pain. We believe that pain and suffering should never be inflicted when it can be avoided. But despite this understanding of animals' sentience, we freely permit and condone wanton cruelty if there is a "valid," specific purpose for it—usually commercial, sporting, or scientific. We castigate the random, gratuitous cruelty of the man who beats his dog or sets fire to his cat, but support the same actions when organized and performed "officially" in the university psychology lab or in military "wound lab" tests. We pride ourselves that the decadent carnage of the Roman Circus Maximus of two thousand years ago is gone, where hundreds of lions and bears were massacred in an afternoon to entertain the bloodthirsty populace. But today, crowds still cheer on the bullfighter, awarding him the bull's ears and tail if he kills elegantly; society men and women still "ride to hounds" to chase and kill the harmless fox (harmless because there are few barnyard chickens left to steal) and wipe its blood on their faces in ancient ritual; hunters still eagerly turn out by the thousands for the yearly deer slaughter; and in Hegins, Pennsylvania, thousands of "sportsmen," women, and children still picnic at the annual Labor Day pigeon massacre, where some eight thousand birds are shot, maimed, stomped, strangled, and killed to the laughter of the jeering crowd.

In our enlightened civilization, we no longer believe animals are machines, as Descartes theorized, but we treat some—the domestic farm animals and the laboratory animals—as though they were. In recognition of animals' sentience, animal welfare laws have been enacted in some countries, but they are not comprehensive and they only require that the animals' most basic needs be addressed. For example, animals should receive food and water, but only at man's convenience (see "Transportation" chapter; the twenty-eight-hour law); they should be properly housed, but only as long as it is not unprofitable to do so (see "Pigs" chapter; the gestation period, and "Calves" chapter; the veal crate); and they should have qualified veterinary care—so farm animals receive daily medication whether they need it or not.

Despite a growing movement towards more humane treatment of animals, man still generally considers his biblically granted "dominion over the beasts of the field and the fowls of the air" as authorization to use animals for his own purposes—his enjoyment, entertainment, scientific enquiry, and food. He does not yet equate dominion with stewardship; he does not recognize his responsibility, reciprocating his privilege as the most powerful life-form on the planet, not to impede, interrupt, or interfere with the inherent evolutionary purposes of other animals.

But, at long last, the traditional view is being challenged. A new paradigm of spiritual, moral, and ethical values is arising. New holistic philosophies, drawn eclectically from ancient and modern sources, see the world and all its life-forms as parts of a greater whole—each part having its own purposes, each fulfilling its own particular evolutionary needs, yet each part belonging, and each deserving respect, compassion, and universal love. We are, in fact, beginning to recognize that all life-forms are interconnected, interdependent, and necessary, like threads in a complex tapestry, where the whole requires the presence of each thread, and each thread is meaningless outside of the whole.

Since Descartes's time, scientists and philosophers have made huge progress in understanding the physical world. We have learned to control and master most day-to-day aspects of the natural world—at least we believe we have. We are convinced we can solve any problem that may arise—given enough time, money, and energy. Yet until recently, man's expanding control over his destiny was limited in one important way. He might explore new frontiers and make revolutionary technological breakthroughs, but radically altering the fundamental concept of life on the planet was inconceivable.

Nuclear weapons, pollution, and exhausted resources have changed all that. Man now has achieved the inconceivable: by an act of will or simply through plain carelessness, he can destroy all life. The recognition of this awful power has dawned in a combination of self-interested fear and outward-looking global concern; it has proven a powerful stimulus to the holistic worldview.

*Christians who close their minds and hearts to the cause of animal welfare and the evils it seeks to combat, are ignoring the fundamental spiritual teaching of Christ himself. They are also refusing the role in the world for which God gave us our brains and our moral sense, to be God's agents to look after the world in the divine spirit of wisdom and love.*

## The Right Reverend John Austin Baker, Bishop of Salisbury

Happily, in light of this new sense of responsibility, man is taking a fresh, closer, and more compassionate look at his relationship with the planet. He is realizing that the conquest of nature is essentially the destruction of nature, that continued tampering with the natural order may eliminate those finely balanced elements that allow life to flourish. Around the world, people are actively working to protect the environment; to save rain forests and fragile, essential tree life; to help feed the millions of hungry and starving people; to prevent the ozone layer from deteriorating further; to free the environment of nuclear and other toxic wastes; and collaborating on a multitude of projects, locally and globally, to keep the earth a life-sustaining place.

A part of this movement involves protecting overhunted animals and saving endangered species from extinction. Whales, gorillas, rhinoceroses, snow leopards, bottlenose dolphins, and California condors are a few on a long and growing list of thousands of species likely to die out. Obviously, losing an entire species reflects badly on our environmental management skills and hurts our generic ego. We care very much about these potential disappearances because the concept of the wholeness of our global system is damaged, and because each lost species makes our world a poorer place. But more importantly, we are outraged that what we once knew to be a part of our inheritance is lost; that we have reached a point where extinctions of species at our hands has become commonplace.

Why is it then, that our "blind spot" for domestic animals prevents us from seeing that the extinction by slaughter of billions of individual farm animals every year—even though they are certainly not in danger of extinction as species—also makes the world a poorer, more damaged place? Perhaps it is because this slaughter is condoned by habit, systematized by tradition, and ignored by generations hardened in childhood against compassion for domestic animals.

Perhaps, in our concern for endangered species, we are moved by the fate of the individual endangered animals themselves—foxes caught in leghold traps, elephants and rhinos killed by the poacher's powerful rifle, dolphins suffocating in indiscriminate fishing nets, or hump-backed whales pierced in the back with explosive harpoons. Why then don't we feel the same compassion for domestic animals? They surely suffer as much as animals in the wild, if not more. If this unselfish, caring concern for the planet is driven as much by compassion for life as by love of nature and the will to survive, then how, in good conscience, can we leave farm animals out of the circle? What kind of a "deal" have we made with our collective conscience that we save endangered species and mass slaughter farm animals?

Compassion for humans and animals is not mawkish, over-emotional sentimentality. Compassion is a noble attribute; it is an expression of the heart and the appropriate response to the suffering of victims of violence. Compassion respects all forms of life and recog-nizes the right of each to fulfill its own purpose. To wish to save a cuddly little pet lamb or a cute baby harp seal from brutal slaughter might be considered sentimental. To wish to prevent all lambs and all seals, cuddly or otherwise, from being slaughtered is an expression of compassion: compassion not just for the animals, but for all life—including the slaughterers. Less violence done is better than more violence done.

A holistic approach focuses attention on the similarities—not just the differences—between humans and animals, especially in physical and biological functions, behavioral needs, and emotions. It is well established that animals feel pain, fear, enjoyment, loneliness, boredom, confusion, excitement, stress, jealousy, and many more common expressions of their intelligence. They avoid discomfort, seek pleasure, and, when healthy, maintain a strong will to live.

There is indisputable evidence of this consciousness, beyond Descartes's machines and the simple "suffering" of Bentham, even though levels of mental and emotional awareness vary between animal species—as they vary among humans. Primates, for instance, can be taught sign language; some use vocabularies of several hundred signs to express joy and sorrow, needs and desires, memories—and a sense of humor. They can even learn to use signs from their companions without human teaching. According to Jane Goodall, the noted researcher of primates, "They are capable of reasoned thought, generalization, abstraction and symbolic representation. They have some concept of self." Goodall further relates that young chimpanzees brought up in human homes and treated like human children, "learn to eat at table, to help themselves to snacks from the refrigerator, to sort and put away cutlery, to brush their teeth, to play with dolls, to switch on the television and select a program that interests them and watch it."

*There is no fundamental difference between man and the higher mammals in their mental faculties. . . . The difference in mind between man and the higher animals, great as it is, certainly is one of degree and not of kind.*

Charles Darwin, *The Descent of Man*

Intelligence and feelings, love of life, and sentience are not limited to humans; there is an overlap between species. So how can we decide who should have a right to life and who should not? Clearly it's not a matter simply of intelligence, or of emotional capacity, or even of soul. According to present human morality, it is a matter of belonging to the human species or not. Because sheep and cattle—even the domesticized little chimp—are animals, and distinct from humans, they can be used, abused, and killed without recourse. The human being grants to himself alone an unequivocal "right to life."

As philosopher Peter Singer points out, a dog or a pig has "a higher degree of self-awareness and a greater capacity for meaningful relations with others than a severely retarded infant or someone in a state of advanced senility," but the dog and the pig have no right to life because the boundary of the right to life is drawn at the boundary of the human species. Yet this dividing line is not watertight.

Humans refuse animals the right to life because animals have no standing in our society. Animals exist without any of the packaging with which civilization surrounds each human, and it is this packaging that determines treatment. Unlike humans, animals appear to have no conscious continuity of culture and no history, no comprehensive social structures such as governments, and no universally accepted and recognized forms of identity like names and known ancestry. Many species do live in groups of varying degrees of organization, from troops of apes to herds of cows and pods of whales, but man is not willing to validate and empower these networks of interconnected relationships. There is nobody to speak for animals; they have no organization, no consensus that they actively promote, and no ability to coordinate retaliation or sanctions against humans who harm them. In the last resort, there is no group of animals or humans to whom man must be accountable for his actions towards animals.

Each human belongs to some kind of group that promotes and protects his or her rights within the framework of society. Each animal, on the other hand, essentially stands on its own, with none of this "packaging" and no group recognized by man to protect its rights. Thus, when an animal comes in contact with man, it can only rely on the goodwill of man for recognition of its rights, and when man chooses to deny or overlook those rights, he is accountable to no one. There is no recourse for the animal, no sanction moral or legal that the animal can invoke. By human standards, animals simply don't count.

To demonstrate the inconsistency of this right-to-life boundary and further indicate the power of accountability—or lack of it—as a factor in the treatment of animals and in the relationship between civilized man and other life-forms, we need only look at the way civilizations of European origin have treated people of color through the centuries. The story is one of total disregard for the right to life, from the enslavement of Africans, once considered a sort of missing link between apes and men; the destruction of the culture of the North American Indians, once perceived as more brutish than the beasts they hunted; and the extermination of the Tasmanian aboriginal tribes in Australia, who just got in the way of new settlers; to the ongoing slaughter and near genocide of Indian tribes in the Amazon basin, whose forests are wanted by powerful commercial interests. These and many similar groups around the world—just like animals—lived outside the bounds of accountability. They have been tortured and killed by the millions—just like animals—with no sanctions imposed on the perpetrators. They did not, and do not, enjoy the protective packaging of so-called civilization. They, too, simply didn't count.

In our society, accountability is a major component in judging the right to life. For the value we place on life has little to do with its intrinsic value, but everything to do with the way life is valued and protected by the irrational, self-serving, and variable rules set by society. The value of a life is man-made and therefore arbitrary. In Roman times, a gladiator's life depended on the mood of the bloodthirsty circus crowd; two hundred years ago, a man could be hanged for stealing a loaf of bread; today, while thousands of Third World children die of starvation each day, there is no limit to the amount of money, equipment, and effort available if one stranded mountain climber needs rescuing in the US. In the Middle Ages, treating an animal as a pet was tantamount to indulging in witchcraft; in India, the cow is considered a sacred animal; today, animal life on a factory farm is reckoned in dollars and cents.

As long as we continue to value life in this erratic, changeable manner, animals and humans who differ from the norm will always be at risk. Their life will always be at the mercy of the whims of the dominant group and not reflect its essential value. Only by standing outside our civilization, only by deliberately crossing a new threshold of appreciation and understanding of the interconnectedness or unity of all life on the planet can we see that another more universal set of rules exists that governs the value of life. Once we observe and understand these, we can incorporate them into our society.

The new paradigm is emerging as inclusive rather than exclusive—all beings are part of the Whole and all have a fundamental right to life. This does not mean there is no difference between killing a human and killing a mouse. It means that being a human does not automatically include the right to kill a mouse. It means that being human is not the exclusive, morally relevant criterion for the right to life. As Singer points out, "we must bring nonhuman animals within the sphere of our moral concern."

The inclusion of animals within this sphere requires that we work out whole new concepts of relationship and interaction between human and nonhuman animals. In the traditional anthropocentric approach, animals are property, while the new mode reflects a radical, uncompromising position: animals exist for themselves, not for humans. We can no longer continue our present malevolence towards other species.

Such a change will certainly bring an upheaval in our daily life—particularly in eating patterns. But it must nevertheless be borne, if we are to encompass animals in this sphere of moral concern. We need a new and broad prescription for practical, day-to-day dealings with other beings—and the first ingredient of that prescription must be compassion.

> *It seemed to me so* right *because the oppression that black people suffer in South Africa—and people of color, women and children face all over the world—is the same oppression that animals endure every day to a greater degree.*

> Alice Walker

The conditions still imposed on animals are similar to those once imposed on slaves and women. Slavery (racism) and the oppression of women (sexism) are expressions of the belief that might means right. Slaves were the personal property of their masters, who exercised over them the power of life and death—without legal or moral recourse. In their lowly status, slaves had no rights. Their owners generally considered them inferior—almost subhuman—and ignored their needs, not as punishment, but because, as it was commonly felt, "they don't have the same feelings as we do." Families were broken up, children sold away, couples separated, beatings administered, and capital punishment inflicted, all to fit the economics and moralities of a certain way of life.

In many male-dominated cultures women have been regarded as no more than chattels and bearers of children—even the existence of their souls was in question. Unwanted girl babies were killed (and still are in some parts of the world); daughters were sold into slavery or marriage; women could not own property; women strictly obeyed husbands or faced severe punishment; and women only recently got the vote in many countries. Even today, in some societies a dowry is still required before a woman can marry, and she may only eat the leftovers, after her husband and his friends have eaten their fill. In the West, the controversy over equal rights and equal pay for men and women continues. The list of historical and current evidence for their inferior status is long, complex, and grim, but only recently has the women's movement around the world made headway against the ingrained prejudice and unfair differential treatment.

Speciesism parallels racism and sexism; it is the perception, as we have touched on, that one species is superior to all the others and therefore has the right to dispose of the others as it sees fit. The justifications for speciesism are as empty as those for slavery and sexism. Man treats animals as inferior beings who have no rights. He is cruel without moral or legal restraint. He disregards or curbs their behavioral needs. He buys, sells, and disposes of them as he wishes. He regards them as factors of economic output. And finally, he kills them at will.

> *. . . Nature in the raw is cruel—of course it is! Animals can indeed be cruel to one another. But we are supposed to be something more than they! Dickensian compassion rescued children from sweat shops. Lincolnian empathy rescued slaves from being "things." Civilization weeps while it awaits one more emancipation.*
>
> Paul Harvey

The abolition of slavery and the emancipation of women anticipate a more compassionate attitude towards animals. Sometime in the not-too-distant future, treatment now meted out to animals will seem as barbaric as the iniquities once suffered by women and slaves. Human beings will take their cue from Leonardo da Vinci who wrote long ago in sixteenth-century Italy, "From an early age I have abjured the use of meat, and the time will come when men such as I will look upon the murder of animals as they now look upon the murder of men."

Isn't it clear that the ongoing holocaust we inflict on nonhuman animals is but another expression of the fundamental cultural mind-set that permits us to continue the nuclear arms race, the commercial deforestation of the rain forest, the pollution of our environment and atmosphere, the existence of worldwide hunger, the death of millions of malnourished children, etc., etc.? When will we begin to see the connections between all these issues?

> *As long as man continues to be the ruthless destroyer of lower living beings, he will never know health or peace. For as long as men massacre animals, they will kill each other. Indeed, he who sows the seed of murder and pain cannot reap joy and love.*
>
> Pythagoras

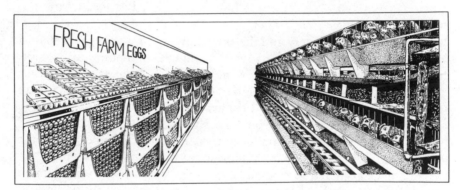

Fig. 46.

# 12

# What You Can Do About It

What you learned as a child and what your child is learning now from children's picture books about the life of farm animals is far from the truth. The popular images of farm life are represented by the gentle and idyllic life on Old MacDonald's farm; they carry the message that life is pleasant and satisfying for the animals in the care of the kindly, amiable farmer—and even if we do finally eat them, at least they have had a good life first.

But this book's photographs of real animals in factory farms are typical too, evidence that all is not well down on the farm. Old MacDonald has been transformed; he is now an agribusinessman and, for farm animals life is a nightmare. For them, fear, distress, illness, and death are the order of the day.

But there are actions that each one of us can take to help alleviate the suffering of these millions of animals, and to reduce the effects of intensive farming on the global food shortage and our deteriorating environment. The task may seem monumental, the opposition immovable, and the mass of people indifferent to our concerns. But, as Mahatma Gandhi once remarked, "almost anything you do will seem insignificant, but it is very important that you do it."

Any action you take, however seemingly inconsequential, will strengthen the movement to relieve animal suffering and slow the abuses of exploitative farming practices. Short of sabotage and radical activism, there are two main approaches to the problem: political action and personal action. For those interested in political action, the best recommendation is to join one of the many organizations in the country concerned with animal rights, farming abuses, and animal experimentation. Most have well-defined political agendas, and ongoing programs of action and lobbying to arouse public interest, to persuade, and to inform. A list of the major groups is included here.

159

Testimonies to the value of public pressure are the outlawing of the veal crate in Britain, the proposed phasing out of laying cages in Switzerland and the Netherlands, and most significantly the broad new farm animal Bill of Rights enacted in Sweden in 1988. This progressive legislation, based on the concept that technology must be adapted to the animals, not the reverse, frees cattle, pigs, and chickens from the abusive confinement of the factory farm, and will serve as a model for other countries.

At a personal level, many people are already aroused and alerted in response to environmental and political anxieties. We send money, we write our politicians, and we support a wide variety of progressive, concerned groups. In fact, we care about the earth because we all have to live here. Now compassion, our essential motivation, must also infuse our knowledge of animal abuse and help in reassessing our attitudes and relationship to animals. We cannot transform the world until we transform ourselves. And the cruelties of factory farming will not go away until we each look anew at our personal responsibility.

If we are truly seeking a life of peace and nurturing concern for the whole planet, we cannot turn a blind eye to the unacceptably cruel treatment and denial of basic rights and behavioral needs meted out to farm animals. As Albert Schweitzer, physician, philosopher, and humanitarian, noted, "Until he extends the circle of his compassion to all living things, man will not himself find peace."

*I hope to make people realize how totally helpless animals are, how dependent on us, trusting as a child must that we will be kind and take care of their needs . . . [They] are an obligation put on us, a responsibility we have no right to neglect, nor to violate by cruelty.*

James Herriot

*We must educate the public. The average person has no idea of what's going on in factory farms, in laboratories, circuses, roadside zoos or rodeos.*

Bob Barker

The place to start reducing the abuse of farm animals is first where we have most contact with them—on the dinner plate—and, second, with our children, who may yet be prevented from acquiring the conventional and conditioned biases of their adult models. Learning that compassion starts with one's own self, children will perhaps no longer permit the cruelties of factory farming to be committed on their behalf.

Thus, while the promotion of vegetarianism is not the aim of this book, a meat-free diet becomes for many the ultimate logical move in the process of learning compassion for animals. Yet, vegetarianism is certainly not the only—or necessary—first step for someone deciding to take personal action against the factory-farming system. If, for example, the medical and health implications have disturbed you, let that be your impetus to act.

The abuses of factory farming stem not just from the eating of meat but from the industry's attempt to satisfy efficiently and profitably an increasing demand for it. There have always been and will always be those who like to eat meat; but the point is, there are many ways to produce it—involving levels of cruelty that range from minimal to horrendous.

Tibetan Buddhists, whose climate and landscape make vegetable growing nearly impossible, eat large amounts of meat—but for religious reasons, they are concerned about taking the life of the slaughtered animal. In order that the fewest lives be taken and the greatest number be fed, they use only the largest animals—their yaks which range freely on the mountain sides until slaughter. Chickens and fish are not eaten because they are small and each life taken feeds only a few people. In addition to this minimal killing rule, Tibetan Buddhists pray before eating it, that the food animal will return to a better life in its next incarnation.

It is curious that animal foods are the only foods subject to religious taboos. Tibetans also seldom eat pork; they consider it unclean, and maintain that it hinders meditation. Orthodox Jews and Muslims also eat no pork, while in addition Orthodox Jews do not mix meat and dairy foods. For those animals they do eat, Jews and Muslims require special—and exceptionally cruel—slaughtering rituals. Hindus who eat meat do not eat beef, since the cow is a sacred animal, and until recently Roman Catholics were not permitted to eat meat on Fridays. Nobody ever said avocados were against the law, or forbade carrots on Mondays.

Money is money. "Laundered" stolen money will buy the same goods and services as "honest" money—but, for most people money earned ethically is preferable to money tainted by crime. Meat is meat. Free-range animals are killed in the same manner as factory-farm animals—but many people, while they enjoy eating meat, have ethical and health qualms about the quality of life an animal enjoys before slaughter. By avoiding "tainted" products, those people can help end the unnecessary, cruel deprivations suffered by factory-farm animals and still eat meat—but "honest" meat.

# Courses of Action

1. Eliminating meat, poultry, eggs, and dairy products from your diet will end your direct support of factory farming, and without question will reduce animal suffering, world hunger, and harmful effects on the global environment. Your health will also improve.

You will not be alone. Millions are already aware of the destructive and ethical implications of a meat-based diet. Britain's population of 65 million, for instance, boasts 1.5 million vegetarians, a figure increasing at roughly 30 percent annually, and in the US there are over 10 million people who consider themselves vegetarians.

As some forty thousand of the world's children die every day from starvation and diseases related to poor nutrition, we might remember that a child growing up eating meat in the West consumes five times as much of the planet's food supply as the child who does not eat meat. If you eliminate meat and poultry from your diet, that's a great start. But don't forget that most eggs come from caged laying hens and that dairy goods are intimately connected to veal production.

2. If #1 seems too radical for you now, search out and buy only meats, poultry, eggs, and dairy goods from non-factory farms. In addition to the ethical benefits, meat from free-living animals generally has more protein and less saturated fat.

These products can be bought from local "organic," "natural," or "health" food stores, food co-ops, and meat suppliers that may operate in your city—check the Yellow Pages—or from farmers and friends in the country. A drive through the countryside can often locate private sellers of free-range, barnyard eggs, and some small country butchers supply meat from range-fed, drug-free animals. Check them out. Locally killed animals will have suffered less from transport-associated disease and injury. But if such products are not available, keep in mind the image of factory-farm life before buying from the supermarket.

3. If you cannot manage either #1 or #2, simply cut down your animal-food consumption.

You will almost certainly get healthier. A British study found that non-meat eaters spent only 22 percent of the time in the hospital that meat-eating people spent there. Animal foods have been linked conclusively to degenerative and other chronic health problems. See the chapter on the medical import of factory farming. Of course, cutting down your meat consumption will reduce animal suffering too.

4. If you continue to eat meat when dining out, know that nearly all restaurant meat, poultry, and dairy goods come from factory farms.

Avoid "premium," "milk-fed," or other fancy veal dishes straight from the veal crate. Avoid also "grain-fed" beef from feedlots, and don't be fooled by "farm fresh eggs." Make restaurants aware of these issues by asking the origin of their foods, and suggesting they find non-factory farm sources. Many restaurants now offer meat-free dishes in response to people wanting less meat, either for health or ethical reasons—thank them for their consideration. You might also seek out and patronize restaurants where no animal foods are sold at all.

*There can be no justification for causing suffering to animals simply to serve man's pleasure or simply to enhance man's lifestyle.*

The Dean of York

5. Learn the sources of all your regular foods and their impact on local and global issues which concern you.

Supporting hunger-relief programs in Third World countries is self-defeating when your own daily diet is contributing to the problem. Nearly all US fast-food chains use Central American beef in their hamburgers; vast areas of rain forest, essential to the ecological balance of the planet, are being laid waste to provide short-term pasture for this cheap beef. Coffee, tea, sugar, and cocoa are grown in Third World countries instead of the staple protein crops needed by their malnourished and hungry populations. These countries' most fertile agricultural land is often exploited by parties whose best economic advantage lies in exporting luxury foods to Western industrialized countries.

6. Get up to date on nutrition so you can eat a healthy diet without relying on meat products.

In a full-page ad in *Life* Magazine in 1955, the American Meat Institute declared, "Trust your instinct . . . you're right in liking meat . . . meat helps everybody acquire and maintain good resistance to many infections. It helps you get more fun out of life—because meat is fun to eat—and because you get more enjoyment out of life when you're enjoying the best of health." Thirty-five years later two-thirds of all deaths in the US—from cancer, stroke, and heart disease—are related to the high fat content of the American diet, and that high fat comes from meat and dairy products. Today, whether you want to lose weight, run faster, train for athletics, or reduce your risk of heart disease, cancer, diabetes, osteoporosis, arthritis, kidney disease, impotence, allergies, and a host of other diet-related diseases, doctors and scientists recommend cutting out foods of animal origin. It is now very important to understand the effects of meat and dairy products on the future health of you and your children.

Recently, the beef industry has been touting beef as "real food for real people," but as Neal Barnard, MD has put it, "if you're a 'real person' eating that kind of 'real food,' you should live real close to a real good hospital, because you are likely to have very real problems."

Read some of the books on nutrition listed in the bibliography. Most of the authors are nutritionists and medical doctors. They are concerned for your health. Beware of nutritional advice from meat-industry sources and some government publications. They are more interested in your pocketbook than in your health.

Millions of healthy productive people around the world eat very little or no meat. The "four essential food groups," those pillars of nutritional advice advocated by the animal-food industry, are myths. They merely encourage high consumption—and hence high sales—of meat, eggs, and dairy products. According to nutritionist Michael Klaper, MD, "The human body has absolutely no nutritional requirement for meat or dairy whatsoever." Plant protein sources provide equally good quality protein with less impact on animal life and the global environment. So eat more grains, vegetables, and fruit. Well-established programs to reduce coronary risk, like the Pritikin Program and the MacDougall Plan, eliminate nearly all animal products from the participant's diet.

7. If you feel overwhelmed by changing your diet overnight, start eating a few meatless meals each week.

With the help of the many excellent vegetarian cookbooks now available—some written especially to help those moving away from meat-based meals—you will enjoy these meat-free dishes and perhaps start to lean away from heavier meat-based foods. Other foods—tofu, miso, and various styles of soy-based vegetable proteins—fill some of the transitional psychological gaps in menu planning. Gourmet and ethnic foods from around the world provide delicious new ideas. Meatless meals never need be boring.

8. As an environmentally aware consumer, support local farmers growing grains, beans, seeds, vegetables, and fruits without chemical fertilizers, with organic methods that nurture the soil, and with natural pest- and weed-control methods.

While many medium-sized farms are disappearing across the US, very small, ecologically minded farms increase in number. They produce food in smaller quantities but in more varieties, and their labor-intensive and sustainable methods contrast with agribusiness's high-energy, massive chemical input techniques of soil management. Low-input sustainable agriculture (LISA) programs are now encouraged by the USDA.

9. Read more about the real welfare of animals.

Informative books, listed here, range from philosophical arguments for animals' rights to studies of factory farming and agribusiness, from books on the health, environmental, and ethical aspects of a non-animal diet to cartoons which force us to reevaluate our conditioned biases.

Some people have spiritual and religious reasons for caring for animals as "our younger brothers." Others believe that before they can change their attitudes to animals—in fact, before they can commit themselves to care—they must prove to themselves intellectually that animals have rights and therefore deserve appropriate treatment at the hands of humans. There are plenty of convincing arguments. Yet, intellectual understanding is not the only valid approach. Intuitively knowing that cruelty to animals is wrong and should be stopped is sufficient reason in itself to change one's actions. Being kind and loving is a state of mind, and it needs no justification if it feels right.

*The fate of animals is of greater importance to me than the fear of appearing ridiculous; it is indissolubly connected with the fate of men.*

Émile Zola

10.  Spread the word.

Every word spoken in animals' defense sows a seed in the listener's mind that can germinate and blossom. Talk to your friends. They will notice your changed food habits and ask questions. Most people don't want to be part of animal suffering, but they just don't know the facts. Our silence must not contribute to their ignorance, and their ignorance must not contribute to animal suffering. Write letters to your legislators and to the media, shedding light on the cruelties of factory farming and demanding change. Raise the issues at political forums. Buy a few stocks in agri-corporations and use shareholder meetings to lobby for the animals.

Again, as an aware consumer, remember that many cosmetics and household products contain slaughterhouse by-products and may be tested on animals for toxicity. At your supermarket search out and ask for "cruelty-free" products—no animal ingredients and no animal testing.

11.  Join the movement to defend animals.

Wherever you live a local group is probably working for improved animal living conditions. If not, there are many national organizations listed in this book. If you cannot be actively involved, send money.

12.  California education law #44806 requires teachers to "impress upon the minds of the pupils the principles of morality, truth, justice, patriotism, and a true comprehension of the rights, duties, and dignity of American citizenship, *including kindness toward domestic pets and the humane treatment of living creatures.*"

Does your state have such a law and is it put into practice? If not, write your local congressman. While on the subject of the law, here are some further ideas for legislation for which you could lobby with your representatives: the provision of funds for educational programs about non-animal diets; the labeling of all products—not just foods and cosmetics—clearly indicating what ingredients, if any, are of animal origin; the provision of alternatives to meat-based foods in all public, school, and institutional feeding programs; the enactment of state laws that will require humane treatment of animals in transit and at auction.

Every voice is needed to counteract the well-financed agribusiness lobby. Our children's education must include discussion of the ethics, exploitation, and humane issues of animal husbandry. While a child's moral values are mostly shaped at home, the school also contributes, and provides important factual background for individual decision making. The meat and dairy industries annually spend millions on educational materials promoting their foods and production methods. As commonly presented in our schools, the industry story is couched in glowing, scientific terms while the negative aspects of modern agribusiness are glossed over. For instance, an American Egg Board publication claims today's "egg-laying facilities" are "actually designed for the welfare of the birds" so that "the birds may be more readily protected from the elements, from disease and from both natural and 'unnatural' (cars) predators [*sic*]." The same publication suggests chickens are debeaked, "to protect the birds from each other" without mentioning that the grossly overcrowded conditions are the chief cause of cannibalistic tendencies. Educational materials giving less than the whole story need balancing with the humane viewpoint.

Does your child's school still teach nutrition using outmoded "four essential food groups" information? This mid-fifties invention of the USDA can be safely forgotten for the nineties. Parents need to know that their children are being taught nutrition in light of the most up-to-date knowledge of the immediate and long term effects of different foods on the human body. Does your child's school still require or encourage dissection of animals? There are alternative experiments available which impart the same knowledge and do not compromise a child's reluctance to cut up animals. Does your child's school offer non-animal foods in the cafeteria? You can help by talking to the school food program director.

13. Teach your children.

The way a child treats animals—whether to fear or to trust them, to be cruel or to be kind, to be indifferent to their suffering or to be compassionate—depends very much on the parent's own attitudes towards animals and on how the parents temper the subtle influences on the child of society at large.

*The perfectly natural compassion and intelligence of the child is seen in its solicitude and love for younger children and especially for small animals, as well as its solicitude for suffering of any kind. . . . Compassionate intelligence is involvement in the other's plight combined with the desire to help in some practical way. Children exhibit this gift quite early, and should, of course, receive every encouragement to exercise it.*

Ashley Montague, *Of Man, Animals and Morals*

Children are born with an innate love for animals and in their early years, they consider animals to be equal to humans. Adults encourage this love by surrounding the child with pets, stuffed animal toys, and picture books of piglets, kittens, and cute furry bunnies. This love is further reinforced by constantly pointing out the animals and birds around us.

Nurturing a love for animals comes easily to us as parents, and our children respond spontaneously and naturally. The difficulty comes in keeping this love alive in the face of opposing pressures and current social mores.

As the early years pass, the child is slowly exposed to the world's discrimination against animals, to adults' callous and indifferent treatment of animals, and to the bewildering concept that some animals (dogs, elephants, and horses) are good while others (coyotes, rats, and snakes) are bad. One day there comes an even more confusing and sometimes-traumatic discovery; many of those animals which are good to love and cuddle, are showing up on the dinner plate, dead, in pieces, and disguised by new and unfamiliar names.

The hardening process accelerates as the child copies the attitudes of those around him. In his innocence, he does not question these inconsistencies which directly negate everything he has previously felt and learned about animals. In many families, God's name is called as the ultimate authority that animals exist to serve us in every way we see fit, that it is proper behavior to kill and eat them.

Finally, the child adopts society's stereotypical, fallacious, and sometimes mythic views towards animals: it's okay to love your dog, until his existence interferes with your life-style—then take him to the pound; it's okay to hunt because man has always hunted, and, if not controlled by hunting, the wild animals will overpopulate and starve; it's okay to experiment on animals because human lives may be saved and humans are more important than animals; it's okay to eat animals because that's why they are here and, anyway, they taste good. He learns to accept the paradoxical axiom that we experiment on animals because they are like us, but we eat animals because they are not like us.

Teaching a child to remain compassionate from his animal-loving infancy to young adulthood is a tough job. He needs guidance and family support to challenge the hardening influences of advertising, television, and today's accepted behavior towards animals. But with warm encouragement, even kids thus hardened can rediscover their compassion.

Often we do not realize that the things we say, do, and buy carry messages to our children about how we value animals. Attending rodeos and buying fur coats clearly express that animals are to be used for our pleasure, even if they must suffer for it. In our culture, it is "normal" to believe that animals exist for our use, indeed that they love to serve us. Advertisements present a happy Foghorn Leghorn, the cartoon rooster, selling us fried chicken products, and show smiling cows lined up to give us their milk. Zoos imply it is acceptable to keep animals caged or enclosed in small spaces, and justify this unnatural incarceration because they say it is "educational" for humans.

Adult—especially parental—hatred and cruelty towards animals can have serious long-term effects on a child's psychological makeup, if the child is taught to follow the adults' example. Echoing St. Thomas Aquinas's injunctions against cruelty to animals for *man's* sake, a study done in cooperation with the Department of Justice, Federal Bureau of Prisons suggests that "a clear relationship" exists between a pattern of substantial childhood cruelty to animals and "a pattern of recurrent violence directed against people."

A small child need not see the horrors of factory farming in order to nurture compassion for animals. An older child, aware some of his food is dead animal flesh, may find this book helpful in making choices about foods and in overcoming the pressures of society. And for adults, the dearly held childhood myths of life on the farm will be replaced with new insights into the invisible world of agribusiness animals. Vital for all is the encouragement, example, confidence, and communication of parents and friends.

Especially do these things with children:

A. Discuss animal issues and include your own values and beliefs. Even the youngest will want to join in.

B. Talk about what it means to be alive—to have life. We are alive and so are animals. All living creatures can experience joy in life, can't they? They can also feel pain.

C. Get children to put themselves in an animal's place. Have them close their eyes and imagine what it would be like to live the life of a veal calf, or a chicken in a cage. Describe the surroundings, the lighting, the noise, the smells, the food, the overcrowding, the restricted movement. Children easily create imagery and can see clearly with the mind's eye. Adults could learn from this technique too.

D. Be aware of which TV programs your children watch and what books and magazines they read. Be ready to talk about the content as far as it affects attitudes to animals and compassion for all life in general.

E. Let your children know that violence and cruelty to animals exist—although they don't need the gory details and pictures. Let them know also how much general ignorance there is about the conditions in which animals are raised, and let them know they can help by talking about it to their friends.

F. Don't make an unwilling or scared child confront an animal. For young children this can create lifelong problems and feelings of alienation towards animals.

G. Children often want pets. Discuss the pros and cons from both your point of view, and from the animal's. Remember, pets may need your care and affection for many years. Be ready to care for unexpected guests such as injured or stray animals. Find out the location of neighborhood animal shelters.

*Life is as dear to a mute creature as it is to a man. Just as one wants happiness and fears pain, just as one wants to live and not die, so do other creatures.*

His Holiness The Dalai Lama

While compassion for animals is important, compassion for humans—even those who don't seem to deserve it—is equally important. Many people with little regard for animals angrily say, "It's either them or us," and "Why don't you spend your efforts taking care of humans instead of animals?" Yet, humans and animals—indeed all life-forms—deserve compassion. As Shakespeare wrote, "The quality of mercy is not strain'd"—and neither is the quality of compassion. Since we create compassion, we can have as much as we need.

# APPENDIX 1

# Ingredients –
# Food and Product Labeling

In the aisles of any supermarket, you can observe shoppers studying the labels of the foods, cosmetics, and household products they are about to buy. They are trying to find out exactly what the product contains, a preoccupation made a little easier by labeling laws that require manufacturers to list all ingredients in foods and cosmetics in order of quantity.

Many foods contain additives that are legal but may for some reason be undesirable to the shopper. Too much salt is harmful, especially to those with heart ailments. Many parents try to reduce their children's sugar intake. Food coloring, preservatives, flavor enhancers, etc., may have long-term carcinogenic effects. For religious reasons, some people study the labels to avoid taboo or forbidden foods or food combinations. Vegetarians and vegans study labels to avoid unexpected animal ingredients.

When it comes to the food they eat, label studiers mostly know what they are looking for. Sometimes, they may reject a certain processed food because of an unknown ingredient with a long chemical name, but mostly the origin of the contents of any labeled food is reasonably clear and easily understood.

But with cosmetics and household products, it is more complicated. Some of the ingredients listed are obvious, but most have chemical or technical names, obscure to the layman shopper. Unfortunately manufacturers of cosmetics, to their relief, are not required to explain what an ingredient is, why it is included, or what its origin is. Who, for instance, knows where sodium lauryl sulfate comes from or why it is a common shampoo ingredient? How many women would rub into their faces a moisturizing cream, advertised as containing placenta, if they knew the placenta belonged to the unborn calf of a slaughtered dairy cow, and that it was ripped out of the dead mother as the fetus lay on the slaughterhouse floor, covered with blood and excreta? For those concerned to avoid products with ingredients of animal origin, the following information should be helpful.

In the food department, it is easy to avoid supporting factory farming by simply not eating meat or poultry. It is harder to avoid dairy products, since these are often "hidden" in cakes, bread, pastas, etc. But if an individual so wishes, boycotting the factory-farming system can go much further than just cutting meat out of the diet. One can attempt to eliminate all the products and by-products of factory farming from one's life, though this becomes more complicated and requires more vigilant investigation because of the technical and trade terminology used.

Animal by-products are now virtually unavoidable—even your car tires may be manufactured with animal-derived ingredients—but that is partly because of the pricing structure of slaughterhouse products in the various industries involved. With fewer animals going through the system, the amount of available by-product will dwindle, and the costs will rise. Eventually, existing non-animal alternatives, which at present are not competitively priced, could fill the gaps in manufacturing raw materials.

To the agribiz industry, there's more to a slaughtered animal than just the meat. A 1,000-pound steer supplies only about 440 pounds of salable cuts of meat. Some of the organs are eaten, but about half the original weight of the steer is not used in the first instance for food. It is sold to a wide variety of manufacturers and, because of the great and constant demand in the US for meat and poultry foods, it provides a ready and relatively inexpensive source of raw materials. Some by-products are obvious. The skins are used for shoes, handbags, clothing, and other leather goods, and we all know that the hooves are made into glue. But very little is wasted; ingredients derived from animals turn up in the most unexpected places.

Many by-products end up in finished goods; others are used in manufacturing processes. Slaughterhouse by-products are found as ingredients in soaps, cosmetics, medicines, perfumes, shaving creams, toothpaste, rubber, plastics, paints, and explosives. Slaughterhouse by-products are used in the manufacture of hydraulic brake fluid, fanbelts, refined sugar, ball bearings, synthetic fibers, and paper. Getting away from products relying on factory farming is almost impossible in this society—even Freon, the gas that keeps your refrigerator cold, uses animal products in its manufacture.

However, few of the animal ingredients have no vegetable or mineral substitutes, and food production is by far the most important stimulus and purpose of the factory-farming system. The by-products are just that—by-products. If food production is reduced by a fall in demand, the industries using by-products will turn to other sources for the chemicals they need.

Many industrial and manufacturing habits have traditionally used animal by-products for many centuries and since World War II, they have had an easy ride, growing alongside the increase in food animal production, taking advantage of the steady and growing supply of raw materials. There are substitutes, however, and basic lifestyles do not necessarily need to change as factory farming is phased out.

The following gives a more detailed explanation of where the various inedible parts of the carcass end up and lists some ingredients of foods and cosmetics available, courtesy of the factory-farming system.

Blood
- dried blood used in feeds for cattle, turkeys, pigs, and other livestock
- liquid blood for pet foods; fertilizer
- pharmaceuticals (thrombin, fibrinolysin, etc.)

Bones, Horns, Hooves, Feathers, and Other Connective Tissue
- glue and adhesives (sandpaper, plywood, paper matches, cardboard, window shades)
- buttons; piano keys; bone china; charcoal pencils
- livestock feeds; fertilizers
- gelatine; photographic film; phonograph records; adhesive tapes; electrical bushings
- marshmallows
- refining: sugar, gold, ball bearings, galavanized steel

Fats
- foods: shortening/lard; oleo; chewing gum; toothpaste
- cosmetics: lipsticks; shampoos; shaving cream; deodorants; soap and detergent; face creams; suntan lotions; etc.
- household goods: crayons and chalk; candles; phonograph records; cellophane; plastics; rubber; linoleum; floor wax and polishes; paint and varnish

- automotive uses: antifreeze; lubricants; brake fluid; car tires; asphalt
- industrial, agricultural, and other uses: printing inks; water repellents; fertilizers; animal feeds; cement; explosives; insecticides; corrosion inhibitors; ceramics; Freon

Glands
- over 130 medicines and pharmaceuticals including: insulin; ACTH/cortisone; glycerine; epinephrine; thrombin; heparin; thyroid extract; glucagon; fibrinolysin; adrenalin; glandular concentrate food supplements

Hair and Hides
- brushes of all kinds: toothbrushes; artists' brushes; etc.
- rug pads; upholstery material; furniture
- shoes; clothing; fashion accessories; luggage;
- air filters; glue; etc.

Intestines and Intestinal Enzymes
- strings for musical instruments; strings for tennis rackets
- sausage casings; coagulants for cheese (rennet and pepsin); beer foam

The following is a list of substances used in foods and cosmetics which nearly always are animal based:

| | |
|---|---|
| Collagen/elastin: | from animal connective tissue |
| Gelatin: | bones, hooves, and other connective tissue |
| Insulin: | pancreatic enzyme |
| Keratin: | horns, hooves, hair, and feathers |
| Lanolin: | sheep's wool |
| Mink oil: | minks |
| Musk: | taken from Asian musk deer; may be reproduced synthetically |
| Pepsin: | pigs' intestinal enzyme |
| Rennet: | calves' intestinal enzyme |
| Stearic acid: | fatty tissue |
| Tallow: | fatty tissue of cattle and sheep |
| Urea, uric acid: | urine |

Listing ingredients derived from animals by name can be tricky because most can be reproduced synthetically. In addition to the above, there are many other ingredients in common use that are by-products of the slaughterhouse, but that are hard to determine by the average label reader. Certainly the best solution for those who wish to avoid slaughterhouse by-products in their everyday lives would be for all foods, cosmetics, household soaps, and cleaners—in fact all products—to be clearly labeled for animal content or animal use in manufacture.

# APPENDIX 2

Addresses of some organizations concerned with Animal Rights and Factory Farming, which can provide information and publications. These are mostly national organizations, but thousands of active local groups doing important work also exist around the country.

## ORGANIZATIONS CONCERNED ESPECIALLY WITH FARM ANIMALS

Animal Rights International
Box 214, Planetarium Station
New York, NY 10024

Animal Welfare Institute
P.O. Box 3650
Washington, DC 20007
(202) 337-2332

Boycott Burger King and McDonalds
Coalition
International Animal Rights Alliance
P.O. Box 1836 GMF
Boston, MA 02205
(617) 734-4068

EarthSave Foundation
706 Frederick St.
Santa Cruz, CA 95062-2205
(408) 423-4069

The Farm Animal, Inc.
P.O. Box 33086
Cleveland, OH 44133

Farm Animal Reform Movement
P.O. Box 70123
Washington, DC 20088
(301) 530-1737

Farm Sanctuary
P.O. Box 37
Rockland, DE 19732

Food Animal Concerns Trust
P.O. Box 14599
Chicago, IL 60614
(312) 525-4952

The Humane Farming Association
1550 California St., Suite 6
San Francisco, CA 94109
(415) 485-1495

The Humane Society of the United
States
2100 L St. NW
Washington, DC 20037
(202) 452-1100

## NATIONAL MAGAZINES

Animals' Agenda
P.O. Box 345
Monroe, CT 06468
(203) 452-0446

Vegetarian Times
P.O. Box 570
Oak Park, IL 60303
(708) 848-8100

Animals' Voice Magazine
P.O. Box 341347
Los Angeles, CA 90034
(800) 828-6423

## ORGANIZATIONS CONCERNED WITH RELIGION AND ANIMALS

Animals Unlimited
5224 Topanga Canyon Blvd.
Woodland Hills, CA 91364
(818) 340-3327

Christians for Animals
7131 Owensmouth, Suite D59
Canoga Park, CA 91303

International Network for Religion
and Animals
P.O. Box 1335
North Wales, PA 19454-0335
(215) 699-6067

Jews for Animal Rights
255 Humphrey St.
Marblehead, MA 01945
(617) 631-7601

## ORGANIZATIONS AND PROFESSIONAL GROUPS CONCERNED WITH MULTI-ANIMAL ISSUES, INCLUDING FACTORY FARMING, LABORATORY ANIMALS, WILDLIFE, FUR ANIMALS, COMPANION ANIMALS, HUNTING, HUMANE EDUCATION, AND ANIMAL PROTECTION LEGISLATION

American Anti-Vivisection Society
Noble Plaza, Suite 204
801 Old York Rd.
Jenkintown, PA 19046
(215) 887-0816

American Fund for Alternatives to
Animal Research
175 W. 12th St., Suite 16-G
New York, NY 10011
(212) 989-8073

Animal Connection of Texas
P.O. Box 679008, Suite 141
Dallas, TX 75367
(214) 373-7867

Animal Legal Defense Fund
1363 Lincoln Ave., #7
San Rafael, CA 94901
(415) 459-0885

Animal Liberation Front Support
Group
1543 N. "E" St., Suite #44
San Bernadino, CA 92405

Animal Protection Institute
2831 Fruit Ridge Rd.
Sacramento, CA 95820
(916) 731-5521

Animal Rights Coalition
P.O. Box 20315
Minneapolis, MN 55420
(612) 822-6161

Animal Rights Information and
Education Service, Inc.
P.O. Box 332
Rowayton, CT 06853
(203) 886-0523

ARM! Animal Rights Mobilization
P.O. Box 1553
Williamsport, PA 17703
(717) 322-3252; (800) CALL-ARM

Association of Veterinarians for
Animal Rights
530 E. Putnam Ave.
Greenwich, CT 06830
(203) 869-7755

Citizens to End Animal Suffering and
Exploitation (CEASE)
P.O. Box 44-456
Somerville, MA 02144
(617) 628-9030

Coalition to Abolish the LD50
Box 214, Planetarium Station
New York, NY 10024

Committee to Abolish Sport Hunting
(CASH)
P.O. Box 43
White Plains, NY 10605

In Defense of Animals
816 W. Francisco Blvd.
San Rafael, CA 94901
(415) 453-9984

Feminists for Animal Rights
P.O. Box 10017
North Berkeley Station
Berkeley, CA 94709

Friends of Animals, Inc.
1841 Broadway, #212
New York, NY 10023
(212) 247-8077

Friends of Animals, Inc.
P.O. Box 1244
Norwalk, CT 06586
(203) 866-5223

Fund for Animals
200 W. 57th St.
New York, NY 10019
(212) 246-2096

International Fund for Animal Welfare
P.O. Box 193
Yarmouth Port, MA 02675
(508) 362-4944

International Society for Animal
Rights, Inc.
421 S. State St.
Clarks Summit, PA 18411
(717) 586-2200

Legal Action for Animals
205 E. 42nd St., #1923
New York, NY 10017
(212) 818-0130

National Alliance for Animal
Legislation
P.O. Box 75116
Washington, DC 20013-5116
(703) 684-0654

National Anti-Vivisection Society
53 W. Jackson Blvd.
Suite 1552
Chicago, IL 60604
(312) 427-6065

(NARN) Northwest Animal Rights
Network
1704 E. Galer
Seattle, WA 98112
(206) 323-7301

People for the Ethical Treatment of
Animals (PETA)
P.O. Box 42516
Washington, DC 20015
(301) 770-PETA

Physicians' Committee for
Responsible Medicine
P.O. Box 6322
Washington, DC 20015
(202) 686-2210

Progressive Animal Welfare Society
(PAWS)
P.O. Box 1037
Lynnwood, WA 98046
(206) 743-3845

Psychologists for the Ethical
Treatment of Animals
P.O. Box 87
New Gloucester, ME 04260
(207) 926-4817

Society for Texas Animal Rights
(STAR)
P.O. Box 595547
Dallas, TX 75359
(214) 821-7047

Theosophical Order of Service
6341 Switzer Lane
Shawnee, KS 66203

United Activists for Animal Rights
P.O. Box 2448
Riverside, CA 92516
(714) 682-7872

World Society for the Protection of
Animals
P.O. Box 190
29 Perkins St.
Boston, MA 02130
(617) 522-7000

## SOURCES OF CRUELTY-FREE PRODUCTS: COSMETICS, HOUSEHOLD CLEANERS, NON-LEATHER GOODS, ETC.

Beauty Without Cruelty U.S.A.
175 W. 12th St., Suite 16-G
New York, NY 10011
(212) 989-8073

Vegan Street
P.O. Box 5525
Rockville, MD 20855
(800) 422-5525

## VEGETARIAN AND VEGAN SOCIETIES

American Vegan Society
P.O. Box H
Malaga, NJ 08328
(609) 694-2887

Jewish Vegetarians of North America
P.O. Box 1463
Baltimore, MD 21203
(301) 366-8343

North American Vegetarian Society
P.O. Box 72
Dolgeville, NY 13329
(518) 568-7970

San Francisco Vegetarian Society
1450 Broadway
San Francisco, CA 94109
(415) 775-6874

The Vegetarian Resource Group
P.O. Box 1463
Baltimore, MD 21203
(301) 366-8343

## SOME OVERSEAS ORGANIZATIONS

*Australia*:

Australian and New Zealand
Federation of Animal Societies
(ANZFAS)
P.O. Box 1023
Collingwood, Vic 3066

Animal Liberation
c/o Environment Centre
102 Bathurst St.
Hobart Tasmania 7000

Animal Liberation
20 Enmore Rd.
Newtown NSW 2042

*Canada:*

ARK II—Canadian Animal Rights
Network
542 Mt. Pleasant Rd., #104
Toronto, Ont. M4S 2M7

Lifeforce
P.O. Box 3117
Main Post Office
Vancouver, BC V6B 3X6

*France:*

Oeuvre d'Assistance aux Betes
d'Abattoirs
10, place Leon Blum
75011 Paris
4-379.11.52

*Spain:*

Alternativa Para La Liberacion Animal
Apartado 38.109
Madrid 28080, Spain

*United Kingdom:*

Animal Aid
7 Castle St.
Tonbridge
Kent TN9 1BH
(0732) 364546

Chickens' Lib
P.O. Box 2
Holmfirth
Huddersfield HD7 1QT
West Yorkshire

Compassion in World Farming
20 Lavant St.
Petersfield
Hampshire GU32 3EW
(0730) 64208
(publishes *Agscene* magazine)

# Illustrative and Photographic Credits

The author and publisher wish to thank the custodians of the illustrations and photographs for granting permission to use them.

# Bibliography
## and Suggested Reading

### A SHORT LIST

Altman, Nathaniel, *Eating for Life*. Wheaton, IL: Theosophical Publishing House, 1977.

Fox, Michael W. *Agricide: The Hidden Crisis That Affects Us All*. New York, NY: Schocken Books, 1986.

Lappe, Frances Moore. *Diet for a Small Planet*, rev. ed. New York, NY: Ballantine Books, 1975.

Mason, Jim, and Peter Singer. *Animal Factories*. New York, NY: Crown Publishers, Inc., 1980.

Moran, Victoria. *Compassion: The Ultimate Ethic*. Rochester, VT: Thorsons Publishing Group, 1985.

Robbins, John. *Diet for a New America*. Walpole, NH: Stillpoint Publishing, 1987.

Wynne-Tyson, Jon. *The Extended Circle: A Dictionary of Humane Thought*. Fontwell, England: Centaur Press, 1985.

### FACTORY FARMING

Fox, Michael W. *Farm Animals: Husbandry, Behavior, and Veterinary Practice*. Baltimore, MD: University Park Press, 1984.

Gold, Mark. *Assault and Battery*. London, England: Pluto Press, 1983.

Harrison, Ruth. *Animal Machines*. London, England: Vincent Stuart, Ltd., 1964.

### ANIMAL RIGHTS PHILOSOPHY

Adams, Carol J. *The Sexual Politics of Meat*. New York, NY: Continuum, 1990.

Fox, Michael W. *Animals Have Rights Too*. New York, NY: Continuum, 1991.

Linzey, Andrew. *Christianity and the Rights of Animals*. New York, NY: Crossroad, 1987.

Linzey, Andrew, and Tom Regan, eds. *Animals and Christianity: A Book of Readings*. New York, NY: Crossroad, 1988.

Masri, Al-Hafiz B. A. *Islamic Concern for Animals*. Petersfield, Hants, England: The Athene Trust, 1987.

Regan, Tom. *The Case for Animal Rights*. Berkeley, CA: University of California Press, 1983.

_____. *The Struggle for Animal Rights.* Clarke's Summit, PA: International Society for Animal Rights, 1987.

Regan, Tom, and Peter Singer, eds. *Animal Rights and Human Obligations.* Englewood Cliffs, NJ: Prentice-Hall, 1976.

Schwartz, Richard. *Judaism and Vegetarianism.* Marblehead, MA: Micah Publications, 1988.

Singer, Peter. *Animal Liberation.* New York, NY: New York Review of Books, 1975.

_____. *Animal Liberation.* 2nd ed. New York, NY: New York Review of Books, 1990.

_____. *In Defense of Animals.* New York, NY: Perennial Library, Harper & Row, 1985.

## HUNGER AND FOOD POLICY

Brown, Lester R., et al. *State of the World, 1987.* New York, NY: W. W. Norton, 1987.

_____. *State of the World, 1988.* New York, NY: W. W. Norton, 1988.

_____. *State of the World, 1990.* New York, NY: W. W. Norton, 1990.

George, Susan, and Nigel Paige. *Food for Beginners.* London, England: Writers and Readers, 1982.

Lappe, Frances Moore, and Joseph Collins. *Food First: Beyond the Myth of Scarcity.* Boston, MA: Houghton Mifflin Company, 1977.

North, Richard. *The Real Cost.* London, England: Chatto and Windus Ltd., 1986.

## NUTRITION AND HEALTH

Barnard, Neal D., MD. *The Power of Your Plate.* Summertown, TN: Book Publishing Company, 1990.

Cox, Peter. *Why You Don't Need Meat.* New York, NY: Thorsons Publishing Group, 1986.

Diamond, Harvey and Marilyn. *Fit for Life.* New York, NY: Warner Books, 1987.

Diamond, Marilyn. *A New Way of Eating.* New York, NY: Warner Books, 1987.

Klaper, Michael, MD. *Vegan Nutrition: Pure and Simple.* Umatilla, FL: Gentle World, Inc., 1986.

_____. *Pregnancy, Children, and the Vegan Diet.* Umatilla, FL: Gentle World, Inc., 1987.

Kushi, Michio. *Cancer and Heart Disease: The Macrobiotic Approach to Degenerative Disorders.* Tokyo: Japan Publications, 1982.

McDougall, John, MD. *The McDougall Plan.* Piscataway, NJ: New Century Publishers, 1984.

Shandler, Michael and Nina. *The Complete Guide and Cookbook for Raising Your Child as a Vegetarian.* New York, NY: Ballantine Books, 1982.

Thrash, Agatha, MD, and Calvin Thrash, MD. *The Animal Connection.* Seale, AL: Yuchi Pines Institute, 1983.

## COOKING

Diamond, Marilyn. *The American Vegetarian Cookbook from the Fit for Life Kitchen.* New York, NY: Warner Books, 1990.

Elliot, Rose. *Vegetarian Dishes from Around the World.* New York, NY: Pantheon Books, a division of Random House, 1981, 1982.

Farthing, Bill. *Odiyan Country Cookbook.* Berkeley, CA: Dharma Publishing, 1977.
Gentle World. *The Cookbook for People Who Love Animals.* Umatilla, FL: Gentle World, 1986.
Hagler, Louise. *Tofu Cookery.* Summertown, TN: The Book Publishing Company, 1982.
Hurd, Frank J. and Rosalie. *Ten Talents Vegetarian Natural Foods Cookbook,* rev. ed. Chisholm, MN: Ten Talents, 1985.
Jaffrey, Madhur. *World-of-the-East Vegetarian Cooking.* New York, NY: Alfred A. Knopf, 1982
Jordan, Julie. *Cabbagetown Cafe Cookbook.* Trumansburg, NY: The Crossing Press, 1986.
Katzen, Mollie. *The Moosewood Cookbook.* Berkeley, CA: Ten Speed Press, 1977.
_____. *The Still Life with Menu Cookbook.* Berkeley, CA: Ten Speed Press, 1988.
Lo, Kenneth H. C. *Chinese Vegetarian Cooking.* New York, NY: Pantheon Books, a division of Random House, 1974.
McDougall, Mary. *The McDougall Health-Supporting Cookbook,* vols. 1 and 2. Piscataway, NJ: New Century Publishers, 1985, 1986.
Robertson, Laurel, Carol Flinders, and Bronwen Godfrey. *The New Laurel's Kitchen.* Berkeley, CA: Ten Speed Press, 1976–1986.
Shulman, Martha Rose. *Fast Vegetarian Feasts.* New York, NY: Doubleday, 1986.
_____. *Gourmet Vegetarian Feasts.* Rochester, VT: Thorsons Publishing Group, 1987.
Thomas, Anna. *The Vegetarian Epicure 1.* New York, NY: Vintage Books, 1972.
_____. *The Vegetarian Epicure 2.* New York, NY: Alfred A. Knopf, 1987.
Tracy, Lisa. *The Gradual Vegetarian.* New York, NY: Dell Publishing Co., 1985.
Wakeman, Alan, and Gordon Baskerville. *Vegan Cookbook.* London, England: Faber and Faber, 1986.

## ON BEING VEGETARIAN OR VEGAN

Akers, Keith. *A Vegetarian Sourcebook.* New York, NY: G. P. Putnam's Sons, 1983.
Braunstein, Mark Mathew. *Radical Vegetarianism.* Los Angeles, CA: Panjandrum Books, 1981.
Giehl, Dudley. *Vegetarianism, a Way of Life.* New York, NY: Harper & Row, 1979
Parham, Barbara. *What's Wrong with Eating Meat?* Denver, CO: Ananda Marga Publications, 1979.
Rosen, Steven. *Food for the Spirit: Vegetarianism and the World Religions.* New York, NY: Bala Books, 1987.
Wynne-Tyson, Jon. *Food for a Future: How Hunger Could Be Ended by the 21st Century,* rev. ed. Wellingborough, Northants, UK: Thorsons, 1988.

## GENERAL

Altman, Nathaniel. *Ahimsa.* Wheaton, IL: Theosophical Publishing House, 1980.
Amory, Cleveland. *Man Kind? Our Incredible War on Wildlife.* New York, NY: Harper & Row, 1974.
Buyukmihci, Nermin, and D. Carol Watson. *Animal Ingredients and Their Alternatives.* Milner, GA: Amberwood, 1982.
Fox, Michael W. DVM. *The New Eden: For People, Animals, & Nature.* Santa Fe, NM: Lotus Press, 1989

Kellert, Stephen R., and Alan R. Felthous. "Childhood Cruelty toward Animals among Criminals and Noncriminals." *Human Relations*, vol. 38, no. 12, New York, NY: Plenum Press, 1985, pp. 1113–29.

Masri, Al-Hafiz B.A. *Islamic Concern for Animals*. Petersfield, Hants, England: The Athene Trust, 1987.

Newkirk, Ingrid. *Save the Animals: 101 Easy Things You Can Do*. New York, NY: Warner Books, 1990.

Progressive Animal Welfare Society (PAWS). *Seattle Peace-Meal Diet*. Lynnwood, WA: PAWS, 1986.

Ryder, Richard D. *Animal Revolution: Changing Attitudes Toward Speciesism*. Cambridge, MA: Basil Blackwell, Inc., 1989.

Schell, Orville. *Modern Meat: Antibiotics, Hormones and the Pharmaceutical Farm*. New York, NY: Random House, 1984.

Sequoia, Anna. *67 Ways to Save the Animals*. New York, NY: HarperCollins, 1990.

Serpell, James A. *In the Company of Animals*. New York, NY: Basil Blackwell, Inc., 1986.

Spiegel, Marjorie. *The Dreaded Comparison*. New York, NY: Mirror Books, 1989.

Vegetarian Society of the United Kingdom Ltd. *International Vegetarian Handbook*. Altrincham, Cheshire, England. Distributed by Thorsons Publishing Group, Rochester, VT. Published annually.

Winter, Ruth. *A Consumer's Dictionary of Cosmetic Ingredients*. New York, NY: Crown Publishers, Inc., 1976, 1984.

_____. *A Consumer's Dictionary of Food Additives*. New York, NY: Crown Publishers, Inc., 1978, 1984.

## MAGAZINES, BROCHURES, AND OTHER USEFUL RESOURCES

*Agscene*, published by Compassion in World Farming, 20 Lavant Street, Petersfield, Hampshire, GU32 3EW, England. (Ten issues per year.) British magazine with news of factory-farming scene in UK and around the world. Coordinates activites to reduce and abolish cruel modern farming and agricultural practices.

*Animals' Agenda*, Box 345, Monroe, CT 06468. (Ten issues per year.) The Animals' Rights News Magazine. Excellent articles, up-to-date overview of national movement, promotes cooperation between groups, and provides a forum for exchange of ideas. Important and worth reading.

*The Animals' Voice*, P.O. Box 341347, Los Angeles, CA 90034.

*Vegetarian Journal*, P.O. Box 1463, Baltimore, MD 21203.

*Vegetarian Times*, P.O. Box 570, Oak Park, IL 60303.